WORDS FROM THE WISE

UNDERSTANDING
AND TRUSTING
OUR GREAT GOD

TIM CHALLIES

GRAPHICS BY JULES KOBLUN

HARVEST HOUSE PUBLISHERS
EUGENE, OREGON

Published in association with the literary agency of Wolgemuth & Associates

Cover and interior design by Studio Gearbox
Cover photo © Creative Travel Projects (scenic image) / Shutterstock

For bulk, special sales, or ministry purchases, please call 1-800-547-8979.
Email: Customerservice@hhpbooks.com

M This logo is a federally registered trademark of the Hawkins Children's LLC. Harvest House Publishers, Inc., is the exclusive licensee of this trademark.

Understanding and Trusting Our Great God
Text copyright © 2023 by Tim Challies
Artwork copyright © 2023 by Jules Koblun
Published by Harvest House Publishers
Eugene, Oregon 97408
www.harvesthousepublishers.com

ISBN 978-0-7369-8581-9 (hardcover)
ISBN 978-0-7369-8582-6 (eBook)

Library of Congress Control Number: 2022944839

Printed in China

23 24 25 26 27 28 29 30 31 / RDS / 10 9 8 7 6 5 4 3 2 1

CONTENTS

INTRODUCTION

Some of my earliest memories are of creeds and catechisms. Parents and pastors alike taught me the truths of the Christian faith and encouraged me to study creeds and the many questions and answers of the catechisms. What a foundation this laid in my young heart!

No words resonated more deeply than the fourth answer of the Westminster Shorter Catechism, which responds to a simple but crucial question: "What is God?" The writers of the Catechism combined sound doctrine with rhythmic, memorable prose to answer thus: "God is a spirit, infinite, eternal, and unchangeable, in his being, wisdom, power, holiness, justice, goodness, and truth." This answer begins with four attributes unique to God, then describes attributes he chooses to share with other beings.

In this book I mean to consider the character of God as outlined in this Catechism, using words from the wise I have collected from a wide variety of Christian writers, preachers, songwriters, and poets.

But first we will remind ourselves of how great thoughts of God ought to lead us to great wonder and delight. For to know God is to love him, and to love him is to have our hearts thrilled by him.

THE SOUL'S DEEPEST THIRST IS FOR GOD

HIMSELF, WHO HAS MADE US SO THAT WE CAN

NEVER BE SATISFIED WITHOUT HIM.

F.F. Bruce

God has made us in such a way that we experience yearnings and cravings. Left to ourselves, we are incomplete and insufficient, feeble and sorely lacking. And though we are often driven and motivated by our physical longings, deeper still are our spiritual longings. Just as we cannot live physically without food and water, we cannot live spiritually without spiritual sustenance. F.F. Bruce says the deepest thirst of all is our thirst for God, and the reason is simple: The God who created us formed us in such a way that we are not meant to exist apart from him. To live apart from God is the spiritual equivalent of trying to live without food and water. It will lead only to weakness, pain, and death. This being the case, may we echo King David, who prayed, "Earnestly I seek you; my soul thirsts for you; my flesh faints for you, as in a dry and weary land where there is no water" (Psalm 63:1). This is a prayer God delights to answer, for he loves to meet our insufficiency with his bounty, our emptiness with his fullness.

God only is the saint's
treasure & chief good;
he lays up treasure in heaven
& this treasure is God.

William Strong

What is it that we, as Christians, long for? What is it that we crave? What is it that will quiet our restless hearts? We want forgiveness, for we know our rebellion. We want joy, for we know our misery. We want justice, for we lament that the righteous suffer while the evil flourish. We want heaven, for we know we deserve hell. There are many longings, many hungers and thirsts, that can drive us to the open arms of the Father. Yet behind them all there is a deeper longing, a brighter treasure, a higher good—God himself. The Bible tells us of a treasure hidden in a field and a man who gave up all he had to buy that field and acquire its treasure (Matthew 13:44). And that treasure is truly God. The greatest longings of our souls cannot be satisfied by forgiveness or joy or justice or heaven or anything else. They can be satisfied only by God, who is himself our treasure, our reward, our joy, our delight, the one without whom we have nothing, and the one with whom we have everything we could ever need.

DELIGHT AND TRUE FAITH
ARE AS INTERWOVEN AS ROOT
AND FLOWER, AS INDIVISIBLE
AS TRUTH AND CERTAINTY;
THEY ARE, IN FACT,
TWO PRECIOUS STONES
GLITTERING SIDE BY SIDE
IN A SETTING OF GOLD.

CHARLES SPURGEON

Christians are often portrayed as downcast and dour, as people who are trapped in a system of beliefs that robs them of joy and life. And with a bit of honest self-examination, we can probably think of times when we have fit the cliché. Yet any fault in this is ours, for as Charles Spurgeon says so well, true faith is meant to be inseparable from deep delight, "as interwoven as root and flower, as indivisible as truth and certainty." God's desire for us is not to live in captivity to a set of rules or to go through religious motions in order to impress him or others. Rather, God's desire is that his love for us, and ours for him, would generate a deep and lasting joy that would make worship a pleasure more than an obligation and make obedience a delight more than a duty. For in coming to know God, we have come to know the most delightful Being there is—the one from whom all true delights flow in an endless fountain. To know God is to find in him great joy and lasting satisfaction.

All our joy must terminate in God;
& our thoughts of God must be delightful thoughts.

It is our duty & privilege to rejoice in God,
& to rejoice in him always;
at all times, in all conditions.

MATTHEW HENRY

There are many faiths in the world and a myriad of gods represented among them. Yet these gods invariably relate to their followers on the basis of works. To honor such gods is to attempt to impress them and, through acts of contrition and obedience, to attempt to gain and maintain their favor. But unlike other gods, the God of the Bible relates to his people on the basis of grace. By his own initiative and through the greatest of all sacrifices, he has won them to himself. And for them the only right and appropriate response is delight—to revel in the knowledge that "God shows his love for us in that while we were still sinners, Christ died for us" (Romans 5:8). The God who gave so much to save us will certainly never turn away from us or do anything that would ultimately harm us. And so at all times and in all conditions, through joys and sorrows, dark valleys and green pastures, great gains and sore losses, we can and must find our joy in the God who has saved us, the God who has brought us safe thus far, and the God who will bring us home to himself.

SPIRITUAL DELIGHT

IN GOD ARISES CHIEFLY

FROM HIS BEAUTY AND

PERFECTION, NOT FROM THE

BLESSINGS HE GIVES US.

Jonathan Edwards

It is right and good to thank God for his gifts. We are to give thanks "always and for everything to God the Father in the name of our Lord Jesus Christ" (Ephesians 5:20). We would be remiss if we failed to thank God for life and health, food and shelter, love and grace. Yet we need to be careful that we do not come to love the gifts more than the giver—to honor God more for what he gives than for who he is. If we wish to truly delight in God, we must not do less than consider his gifts, but do more—we must consider God himself. For the deepest spiritual delight comes not from pondering the things God has given us, but from meditating upon who God is. It is when we ponder his beauty and perfections, his essence and character, that we come to appreciate him most, to find wonder and awe in him. "If the wicked love God, it is only for his benefits," said Henry Smith.[1] But God's children love him because he is so lovable—so perfectly worthy of our delight.

THE LARGER THE ISLAND OF KNOWLEDGE, THE LONGER THE SHORELINE OF WONDER.

RALPH W. SOCKMAN

If you wished to search for driftwood or seashells or sea glass, you would do well to visit the coast at the point where the beaches are longest, for the longer the shoreline, the greater the likelihood of finding what you seek. And in this author's metaphor, the likelihood of finding delight in God is directly proportional to our knowledge of God. If we know little about God, there is little to spark awe within us. But if we know much about God, we will inevitably find much that causes us to marvel at who he is. This puts on each of us the responsibility to know God as he is, to study what he has revealed of himself through nature—where "the heavens declare the glory of God, and the sky above proclaims his handiwork" (Psalm 19:1)—and what he has revealed of himself through the Bible—where we learn that "the precepts of the LORD are right, rejoicing the heart" (Psalm 19:8). To know God is to delight in God, and to know God more is to delight in God more, for the scope of our wonder depends upon the span of our knowledge.

Our joy in God is insatiably greedy.
The more you have, the more you want.

THE MORE YOU SEE, THE MORE YOU WANT TO SEE.

THE MORE YOU FEEL, THE MORE YOU WANT TO FEEL.

John Piper

The renowned missionary David Brainerd once described a fascinating spiritual realization: "When I really enjoy God, I feel my desires of Him the more insatiable and my thirstings after holiness more unquenchable."[2] He had discovered that delight causes a kind of cascade effect where the more he had, the more he craved. Though his enjoyment of God satisfied him in one sense, it left him with an even deeper longing in another. John Piper makes a similar observation, going so far as to label our joy in God as a good and noble kind of greed. Like any other form of greed, it cannot be sated, but always longs for more. And this is just as God intended it, so that the closer we draw to him, the closer we long to be, and the more joy we find in him, the more joy we long to experience. We never fully arrive on this side of heaven and are never fully satisfied, but always long for the fullness of joy that will be ours when we are finally face-to-face with the one we love.

Nothing else under the sun can be as dry, flat, tedious and exhausting as religious work without the wonder.

Vance Havner

If we are meant to find great joy and true delight in God, why is it that some religious people appear so joyless? Why are there some who seem to do little more than go through the motions of religion but without any spirit, any zeal, any fervor? Vance Havner points us in the right direction when he writes of work that is without wonder. Our service for God will either come out of an understanding of grace or an assumption of merit. We will either work *from* the favor of God or *for* it. And nothing will prove more discouraging than losing the wonder of grace and instead laboring to try to win the favor of God. It is grace—unmerited divine favor—that kindles our joy, and it is grace that keeps the fires burning warm within our hearts. "A true believer looks on religion, not as a burden which he must be forced to endure, but a privilege which is his happiness to enjoy," says Andrew Gray.[3] It can be enjoyable and bring happiness to our souls only as long as it is marked and motivated by grace.

EVERYTHING WE SAY OR DO WILL EITHER
ILLUMINATE OR OBSCURE THE CHARACTER OF GOD.
SANCTIFICATION IS THE PROCESS OF JOYFULLY
GROWING LUMINOUS.

Jen Wilkin

When we decide to become followers of God, we automatically align ourselves with God. When we profess faith in him, we become visible representatives of an invisible God. Our lives, our words, our actions all begin to say "This is what God values," and "This is what God is like." It falls to us to understand the character of God and then to display it in the way we live. We ought to be wise in order to show that God is wise; we ought to be just in our dealings with others because God is always just in his dealings with others; we ought to be good and loving and merciful because God is good and loving and merciful. As Wilkin says, "Everything we say or do will either illuminate or obscure the character of God." Our lives will speak truth about God insofar as they are consistent with his character, and they will speak lies about him insofar as they are inconsistent with his character. Our task is to grow luminous—to shine the light of God's character in a dark world.

WHOM ELSE DO
YOU KNOW THAT IS
HIGH, YET HUMBLE;
STRONG, YET SENSITIVE;
RIGHTEOUS, YET GRACIOUS;
POWERFUL, YET MERCIFUL;
AUTHORITATIVE, YET TENDER;
HOLY, YET FORGIVING;
JUST, YET COMPASSIONATE;
ANGRY, YET GENTLE; (AND)
FIRM, YET FRIENDLY?

Sam Storms

None of us is perfect, none of us complete, none of us without weakness and sin. For that reason, none of us perfectly exemplifies godly character. Though we may have grown in humility, we will still at times take advantage of people we are meant to lead with love. Though we may value mercy, we will still be tempted to overwhelm or even abuse others with our strength. Though we may display the blessed virtue of gentleness, we will still at times succumb to outbursts of anger. God, and God alone, perfectly exemplifies every virtue in its fullest form. He is high and humble, strong and sensitive, righteous and gracious, powerful and merciful, authoritative and tender, holy and forgiving, just and compassionate, angry and gentle, firm and friendly—all of these in perfection, each of these without ever diminishing the others. He is a God who is worthy of our praise, our adoration, our delight. In the pages that follow, we will get to know this God—to know him in his being, wisdom, power, holiness, justice, goodness, and truth. And as we come to know him, we will inevitably and wondrously delight in him.

GOD IS

The Catechism describes God through two different lists of attributes. God is (1) infinite, eternal, and unchangeable, in his (2) being, wisdom, power, holiness, justice, goodness, and truth. It is important to understand that each of the attributes from the first list applies to each of the attributes in the second. Hence, God is infinite in his being (and infinite in his wisdom, power, holiness . . .), he is eternal in his being (and eternal in his wisdom, power, holiness . . .), he is unchangeable in his being (and unchangeable in his wisdom, power, holiness . . .), and so on.

When we refer to God's *being*, we refer to his existence, to his nature, and to the qualities of his "Godness." And from the Catechism we know that his being is infinite (unlimited in extent or degree), that it is eternal (without beginning and without end), and that it is unchangeable (unable to be altered in any way). God exists everywhere and at all times; he has always existed and will always exist; he is unchanging and, indeed, unchangeable by any power, any fact, any circumstance. Let's consider the being of God and marvel together at who he is.

The ultimate fact
about the universe is
a personal God.

PETER C. MOORE

There must be a starting point for all knowledge. There must be some ultimate fact that lies at the very foundation of all we know, all we believe, all we insist upon as being true. The Bible's opening words establish this fact: "In the beginning, God . . ." (Genesis 1:1). At the beginning of history as we know it, at the dawning of the universe, at the first moment of time, God already was. There was never a time he had been formed or made, never a time he did not exist. He is eternal and uncreated, infinite and self-existent. He is also personal, and thus not a mere force, energy, or power, but an authentic being. As a being, he is one in essence, one in will, but three in persons—Father, Son, and Holy Spirit. As a being, he can speak and act, create and command, love and hate, save and judge. And as a being, he can have relationships with other beings that are personal, intimate, and genuine. Thus, the ultimate fact about the universe—and the ultimate fact that makes sense of the universe—is a personal God.

God exists.
He exists as He is
revealed by the Bible.

The reason one must
believe that He exists
is because He said
that He exists.

JOHN MACARTHUR

We have seen that "the ultimate fact about the universe is a personal God." But how do we know this to be true? How do we know that this personal God actually exists? Theologians have offered many methods through which we can have confidence that there is a God, some of them by focusing on the existence of order in the universe, others on the existence of morality in humanity, and still others on the existence of a deep spiritual longing within the human heart. Each of these is said to prove that God exists and to put a moral imperative on us to believe. Each of these methods has its own strengths, but most ultimately, we must believe God exists because he has told us so. God has revealed his existence, his character, and his actions through the words of sacred Scripture, and we are under obligation to believe him. Because he has spoken, we have no excuse to deny that there is a God, to deny that he has created us, and to deny that he relates to us personally. We know he exists because he has told us he exists. It's really as simple as that.

God is not for proof but proclamation; not for argument but acceptance.

ROBERT M. HORN

Is it possible to prove that God exists? Is it possible to prove this so definitively that human beings must quiet their minds, bow their knees, and submit their hearts to him? Robert Horn reminds us that we can so easily lose our way and allow good motives to distract from our God-given purpose. God does not tell us to go into the world and convince others of his existence. He does not command us to engage in arguments and disputes about whether he does or does not exist. Rather, he commissions us to go and "make disciples of all nations, baptizing them in the name of the Father and of the Son and of the Holy Spirit, teaching them to observe all that I have commanded you" (Matthew 28:19-20). Our God-given task is to proclaim the gospel of God and to call upon people to accept it—to believe the good news of salvation by grace through faith in Christ Jesus. As we do so, we trust that God himself will bring conviction of his existence and submission to his purpose.

The existence of God does not just face us with **something** to be believed or rejected, but ***someone*** to be accepted or rejected.

Peter S. Williams

It is good and necessary to believe that God exists, but it is also insufficient. After all, "Even the demons believe—and shudder" (James 2:19). Satan himself has stood in the presence of God and has not the least shred of doubt about his existence. Yet he continues to lead the rebellion against him, continues to attempt to steal God's glory for himself. Thus, as we awaken to the existence of God, we must do more than give assent to the fact of it. And that's because God is not merely some*thing* but some*one*. God is not a fact to be believed or rejected, as we may choose to believe or reject disputed facts of science or history. Rather, God is a being who must be either accepted or rejected. For God is not interested in our assent but our reception. His desire is not merely that we would believe he exists, but that we would put our faith in him and enter into a living, vital, and deeply personal being-to-being relationship where we relate to him as children for whom their father has deep love and deep delight.

IF YOU'RE SINCERELY
SEEKING GOD, GOD WILL
MAKE HIS EXISTENCE
EVIDENT TO YOU.

WILLIAM LANE CRAIG

In ancient times, God made this promise to his people: "You will seek me and find me, when you seek me with all your heart. I will be found by you, declares the LORD" (Jeremiah 29:13-14). Though that was a promise made to a specific people in a specific context, it powerfully displays God's tender heart. God turns away none of those who come to him with empty hands and a broken heart, none of those who come to him with a humble sincerity. Later, Jesus said, "All that the Father gives me will come to me, and whoever comes to me I will never cast out" (John 6:37). He tells us that the people who are loved by God will inevitably come to God, find acceptance, and be held safe forever in his unbreakable grip. What's more, God waits patiently, for it is not his will "that any should perish, but that all should reach repentance" (2 Peter 3:9). The reason God gives us knowledge of his being is so we can respond to the wonder and beauty of it, so he can save us by his mercy and grace.

MEN AND WOMEN WHO REFUSE TO **ACKNOWLEDGE GOD'S EXISTENCE DO SO,** IN THE FINAL ANALYSIS, BECAUSE IT IS **CONTRARY TO THEIR MANNER OF LIVING.** THEY DO NOT WANT TO BOW **TO THE MORAL CLAIMS OF A** HOLY GOD ON THEIR LIVES.

R.C. Sproul

R.C. Sproul makes a bold claim here. He insists that those people who utterly reject the existence of God—not just any god, but the God of the Bible—do not do so ultimately on the basis of insufficient proof or inadequate arguments (even if that is their insistence), but on the basis of moral rebellion. They ultimately reject God because to admit his existence would be to admit his being, and to admit his being would be to admit his right to rule over them. If God exists as a personal and present being, then they live in a world fashioned according to his mind and governed according to his law. And they, like all of us, prefer to be a law unto themselves. Rather than bow the knee, they shake the fist; rather than praising his name, they deny his existence. Rather than submitting to God, they elevate themselves to rule over God. They reject the one who made them and the one who is so willing to save them.

GOD IS THE FIRST, MOST CHIEF, AND MOST PERFECT BEING FROM WHOM THERE FLOWS AND DEPENDS ALL ENTITY AND PERFECTION.

PETER DU MOULIN

God is the first being—the one who preexists all others and who, in fact, has no beginning and no end. He has always been and will always be. God is the chief being—the one who is preeminent over all others and who can never be superseded or ultimately contradicted. God is the most perfect being, who is without limit and blemish in each and every one of his attributes, in each and every one of his deeds, desires, and commands. Because God is first, chief, and perfect, all other being—all entity—flows from him and is moment-by-moment dependent upon him. Whatever else in this world may be perfect and unblemished, it is that way only because it is made by God, because it resembles God, and because it is kept unblemished by God. He is the source of all that exists, all that is good, all that is perfect and wonderful. Whatever blessings you enjoy today, you can be certain that their most ultimate source is this great and powerful God.

THERE IS BUT ONE GOD,
THE MAKER, PRESERVER AND
RULER OF ALL THINGS, HAVING IN
AND OF HIMSELF, ALL PERFECTIONS,
AND BEING INFINITE IN THEM ALL;
AND TO HIM ALL CREATURES OWE
THE HIGHEST LOVE, REVERENCE
AND OBEDIENCE.

James Boyce

There is but one God who exists in the Trinitarian relationship of Father, Son, and Holy Spirit, each of these persons coequal and co-eternal. God made all things, he preserves all things, and he rules over all things—all creatures, all matter, all time, all space, all actions, all decisions, all . . . everything. In and of himself—without reference to any other being—God has all perfections and is infinite in them all, which means that as we consider God's wisdom, God's power, God's holiness, justice, goodness, and truth, we must understand that God is infinite, eternal, and unchangeable in each of them. Though each of these qualities is distinct, each of them also impacts the others, so that God's wisdom, for example, is exercised in his power, holiness, justice, goodness, and truth. God, being who he is and what he is, is worthy of our love, reverence, and obedience—and not just worthy of it, but deserving of it. The only right response to a God like this is to bow the knee to him and worship him with our hearts, our mouths, our very lives.

The true name of Being is proper to God only;
the creatures are in themselves but
shadows & appearances of beings.

God alone is.

_____

Thomas Goodwin

Each human is a being. God is a being. But there is a crucial distinction between our being and God's: God's is self-existent but ours is created. God is the one and only whose being exists before and beyond and outside of what has been created. He is the Alpha and the Omega, the first and the last, the beginning and the end, the One who is without creation or creator, the One who exists by his own will alone, the One who has always been and will always be. And while we, too, have being, ours is finite, limited, dependent, created, and mortal. Our existence is derived from God's, since "In him we live and move and have our being" (Acts 17:28). Our being, compared to God's, is like molehills are to mountains, as puddles are to oceans, as fireflies are to stars in the night sky. Or as Thomas Goodwin says, as a shadow is to the object that casts it—no less real, but only a pale, imperfect imitation. True Being belongs only to the One who has always been and will always be.

God exists in himself & of himself.
His being he owes to no one.
His substance is indivisible.
He has no parts but is single
in his unitary being.

A.W. TOZER

We tend to learn new things by drawing comparisons to things with which we are already familiar. If we want to explain what an e-book is, we might first describe a printed book, then distinguish it from the electronic equivalent. If we are asked to describe Diet Pepsi, we might tell how it is different from regular Pepsi or from Diet Coke. Thus, new knowledge tends to be derived from existing knowledge. Our temptation when attempting to better understand God is to begin with ourselves, then to tell how God is different from us. And while this can be helpful, it reverses the proper order, for it is we who are the derived beings. God is not just more than a human being and not just a bigger and better version of humanity. Rather, God is a being of a completely different order and one who is utterly unique from all else that is. Though God shares some of his attributes with us, his being is as different from ours as day is from night and sand is from water.

We trust
not because
"a god" exists,
but because
this God exists.

C.S. LEWIS

Lewis makes a distinction here that is both plain and profound, that is simple, yet of the highest significance. There is all the difference in the world between "a god" and "this God," between any god and the God of the Bible. Christians are not mere theists, people who demand the existence of some god or who would be satisfied with any god. Our eyes have not been opened and our hearts made receptive to the existence of the first higher power we have heard of or the one we regard as most persuasive. No, our longings have led us to *this* God, to the true God, the only God. If we had not found him, we would be searching still. If he had not satisfied us, we would be restless still. If we had not found joy in him, we would be discontented still. Our trust is not in the notion of a god or the existence of some kind of god. No, it is fixed on the God who has revealed himself to us persuasively and personally as the God who is, the God who lives, the God who loves.

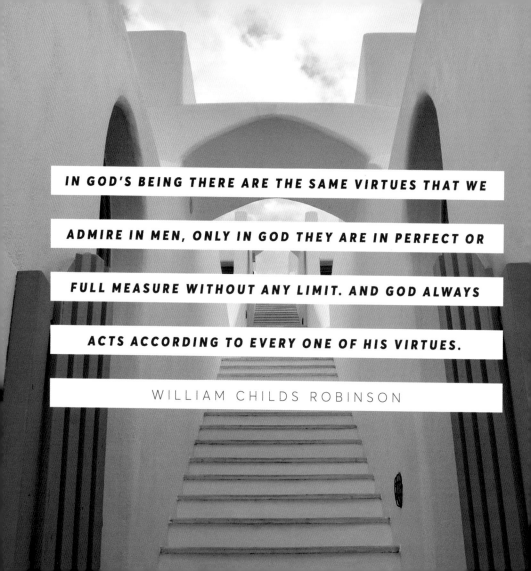

IN GOD'S BEING THERE ARE THE SAME VIRTUES THAT WE ADMIRE IN MEN, ONLY IN GOD THEY ARE IN PERFECT OR FULL MEASURE WITHOUT ANY LIMIT. AND GOD ALWAYS ACTS ACCORDING TO EVERY ONE OF HIS VIRTUES.

WILLIAM CHILDS ROBINSON

There is much to admire in human beings. Because we are made in the image of God, we can imitate God—we can love and rejoice, invent and create, make peace and grant grace, display mercy and extend pardon. We can display a host of precious traits of character and do a world of good. Yet all the while we remain aware that "the best of men are but men at best." The best of us have failures that tag along with all our successes, sins that accompany all our graces, vices that mix with every virtue. The humblest is still at times prideful; the most gracious is still at times practically barbaric. In God and God alone do we see virtues that are unalloyed by iniquity, goodness that is untouched by any ill motive. At all times and in all circumstances, God acts according to all his virtues and abilities so that he is never more or less wise, never more or less powerful, never more or less holy, good, just, or true. As we continue to delight in the God who is, let's consider each of these precious virtues.

GOD IS
WISE

We value wisdom and give honor to those we count as particularly wise. Every culture has had its sages, its philosophers, its wise men, its people who stand above the rest in their wisdom. But perhaps it would do us good to consider what wisdom actually is. To be wise, we must have access to information and then be able to properly assess and interpret that information so it becomes what we call knowledge. Wisdom is then applying our knowledge to the practical matters of life and existence. Thus, wisdom is about living well—about applying information and knowledge to life's joys and sorrows, blessings and challenges. Most ultimately, wisdom is about living out God's purposes for the people made in his image.

According to the Bible, wisdom is inseparable from a right understanding of God. To be wise is to fear God, to know him as infinitely, eternally, and unchangeably wise, and to see his wisdom displayed in creation, in providence, and in his marvelous work of redemption. Those who know him will begin to think as God thinks and thus act in the ways he means for us to act. Those who know God as wise will themselves gain his wisdom. In the pages to come, let's consider God's wonderful wisdom and how, through his grace, it can be ours.

WISDOM IS THE
RIGHT USE OF KNOWLEDGE.
TO KNOW IS NOT TO BE WISE.
MANY MEN KNOW A GREAT DEAL, AND
ARE ALL THE GREATER FOOLS FOR IT.
THERE IS NO FOOL SO GREAT A FOOL
AS A KNOWING FOOL. BUT TO
KNOW HOW TO USE KNOWLEDGE
IS TO HAVE WISDOM.

Charles Spurgeon

Wisdom depends upon knowledge because, as Spurgeon tells us, wisdom is the right use of knowledge. Of course, not all knowledge is used rightly, which is why there are many people in this world who are extremely well-informed but also extremely foolish. "There is no fool so great a fool as a knowing fool." Wisdom is displayed in applying knowledge to plans and purposes, to challenges and circumstances, so that they advance the best and highest goals. A person who has no knowledge can only ever act in ways that are unwise. A person who has limited knowledge will sometimes act in ways that are wise and sometimes in ways that are unwise. But a God who has all knowledge can be relied upon to act in ways that are truly and fully wise. "To know how to use knowledge is to have wisdom," and God displays his wisdom in having perfect knowledge and then deploying it in the wisest ways and toward the wisest purposes.

Because God knows
all things perfectly, He knows
no thing better than any other
thing, but all things equally well.
He never discovers anything.
He is never surprised, never
amazed. He never wonders
about anything nor . . . does
He seek information
or ask questions.

A.W. TOZER

"Folly is bound up in the heart of a child," says Solomon (Proverbs 22:15), and the great task of parenting is to lead children from foolishness into wisdom—to teach them knowledge and to instruct them in how to practically apply it to life. Hence the great cry of Proverbs is "Get wisdom; get insight; do not forget, and do not turn away from the words of my mouth" (Proverbs 4:5). But while we and our children gain knowledge slowly and only with much effort, God never gains and never loses it. While we know some things well and other things poorly, God knows all things with perfection. Nothing ever occurs to God, nothing ever baffles or confuses God, nothing surprises him. There is nothing he needs to clarify, no information he needs to learn, no data he needs to seek. He knows all things equally well, which is to say, perfectly well. And the natural consequence of perfect knowledge and perfect motives is perfect wisdom.

GOD DOES NOT REMOVE HIS **THOUGHTS FROM ONE THING TO** ANOTHER, BUT SEES ALL THINGS **ALTOGETHER UNCHANGEABLY.**

MATTHEW NEWCOMEN

Though we may like to consider ourselves capable multitaskers, the fact is we can really only *do* one thing and *think about* one thing at any given moment—at least if we wish to do things well and to think with clarity and insight. If we wish to meditate on God and his Word, we must force ourselves to stop thinking about our tasks and problems and circumstances. If we wish to set facts within our memory, we must get away from the hustle and bustle of life so we can focus, concentrate, and memorize. But God is not limited in this way. His thoughts do not flit about and are not constrained to focus on only one thing at any one moment. The perfection of his knowledge is not just in its extent but also in its ability. He does not merely know all things, but also knows and recalls all things at every moment. Therefore, he never acts on anything less than a full knowledge of all the facts, for they are all before him at all times.

Wisdom is the *power to see*,
and the *inclination to choose*,
the *best* and *highest goal*,
together with the *surest
means of attaining it*.
Wisdom is, in fact, the
*practical side of
moral goodness*.

———————————

J.I. PACKER

We have learned that wisdom is the right application of knowledge and that, in God's case, wisdom is the perfect application of perfect knowledge. Such an understanding of God's wisdom ought to give us great comfort, for as J.I. Packer tells us, "Wisdom is the power to see, and the inclination to choose, the best and highest goal, together with the surest means of attaining it." God's wisdom is not directed at mediocrity or second best. He does not mean to accomplish purposes that are just okay or merely good enough or making the best of a bad situation. Rather, God's perfect wisdom leads to the perfect attainment of perfect purposes. His wisdom is directed at accomplishing the absolute highest and best goals and accomplishing them through the absolute highest and best means. The consequence for us is that just as we can have confidence in God's ends, we can have every bit as much confidence in his means, for it is through his wisdom that he enacts his goodness.

HE FORMED THE STARS, THOSE HEAVENLY FLAMES,

HE COUNTS THEIR NUMBERS, CALLS THEIR NAMES;

HIS WISDOM'S VAST, AND KNOWS NO BOUND,

A DEEP WHERE ALL OUR THOUGHTS ARE DROWNED.

Isaac Watts

God's wisdom is not something that he maintains merely within his mind, but something that he displays outside of himself—through creating the world, through sustaining and governing the world, and perhaps most ultimately through achieving redemption for the world. In these rhythmic lines, the great hymn writer Isaac Watts calls on us to look to what God has made, especially to the night sky with its boundless expanse and glittering stars, and to see there "a deep where all our thoughts are drowned." By studying God's creation—in its majesty, its intricacy, its creativity—we see that it cannot have come into being by itself, without the hand of a Creator. Rather, it must have been designed by a mind that is vast and wise and established by a power that is unbounded and unlimited. The more we look at creation and study it in awe, the more we must see and know the majestic wisdom of God and the sheer weakness of mankind.

God did not consult
us in making the world,

yet it is well made;

why should we expect then
that he should take his
measures from us in
governing it?

Matthew Henry

Each of us is prone at times to lose our confidence in God's wisdom and to assume that he would benefit from a bit of our own. How often do we grumble and complain against God's will? How often in prayer do we attempt to direct God according to our own limited knowledge, our own limited wisdom? Yet God's creation has a way of redirecting our thoughts, for it displays the greatness of his wisdom. God created it without the least bit of input from any man, yet he made it good—and very good. And if God exercised his wisdom in creating so wonderful a universe, shouldn't we trust him to exercise his wisdom in the affairs and circumstances of our lives? Will we trust him with creation but not providence, trust him to create but not to direct? To ask the question is to highlight its absurdity. Faith directs us to believe that God's providence is every bit as beautiful as creation—as beautiful as the mighty mountains, as awesome as the expanse of the oceans, as stunning as the most wondrous of all the creatures that live on the earth.

PROVIDENCE IS
USUALLY EXERCISED
IN CONTRARIES;
IT IS THE DIVINE METHOD
TO HUMBLE, THAT HE MAY
EXALT; TO KILL, THAT HE
MAY MAKE ALIVE;
TO BRING LIGHT OUT
OF DARKNESS AND
HELL OUT OF HEAVEN.

Francis Raworth

The Bible is full of wonderful paradoxes, statements that seem to contradict one another, but that actually highlight the fact that God's wisdom is so very different from our own. Hence, we learn that humility is the way to greatness, that riches are the way to poverty, that a cross is the way to a crown of glory. God's providence often leads in directions that seem surprising, discomforting, even agonizing. Yet this should not shock us. God's wisdom is much higher than our own, so his methods are also much different from our own. "My thoughts are not your thoughts, neither are your ways my ways, declares the LORD. For as the heavens are higher than the earth, so are my ways higher than your ways and my thoughts than your thoughts" (Isaiah 55:8-9). God thinks higher thoughts, exercises deeper wisdom, and acts with greater intentionality. He knows how to bring about his great and glorious purposes, and it falls to us to trust, submit, and await the time when the full picture will be revealed.

God's secrets, mysteries, and purposes were all darkly veiled until the Son of God appeared and opened up the wisdom of the Father to us.

Mark Jones

God's wisdom is displayed in his acts of creation, providence, and redemption. God's wisdom is also personified. In the book of Proverbs, wisdom is often equated with a human being, a woman who is crying out for people to hear and heed her instructions. "Does not wisdom call? Does not understanding raise her voice? On the heights beside the way, at the crossroads she takes her stand; beside the gates in front of the town, at the entrance of the portals she cries aloud: 'To you, O men, I call, and my cry is to the children of man. O simple ones, learn prudence; O fools, learn sense'" (Proverbs 8:1-5). Then, when God's timing was right, he sent his Son into this world as Wisdom himself, as the One who would perfectly and definitively unveil God's plans and unfold God's purposes. The wisdom of God was displayed in the coming of the Lord Jesus Christ, who would explain how to live wisely and who would display a life that was perfectly directed at the good of others and the glory of God.

HOW WONDERFUL AND
UNSEARCHABLE IS THAT
WISDOM THAT BY THE FALL OF
MAN RAISED HIM TO A GREATER
HEIGHT OF HAPPINESS THAN
EVER HE HAD BEFORE?

Patrick Gillespie

The greatest of all displays of God's wisdom is in redemption—in saving a people to himself. God had created humanity good and sinless, made in his image to praise and honor him. But humanity turned away, scorning God and preferring to be their own gods. God could have left us on our own. He would have been within his rights to give us justice without grace, wrath without mercy. But in love he wished to save us, and in his wisdom he knew how to ensure that sin would be punished and sinners saved. And so he sent his Son into this world to fulfill the law by living an unblemished life, and then to pay for sin by suffering an atoning death. But death could have no claim on one who had committed no sin, so he was gloriously raised from the dead. From the greatest evil came the greatest good; from the greatest fall came the greatest rise; from the greatest grief came the greatest happiness. And the origin of it all was the wonderful wisdom of God.

GOD WILL NOT ONLY BE ADMIRED BY HIS SAINTS IN GLORY
FOR HIS LOVE IN THEIR SALVATION BUT FOR HIS WISDOM IN
THE WAY TO IT. THE LOVE OF GOD IN SAVING THEM WILL BE
THE SWEET DRAFT AT THE MARRIAGE FEAST, AND THE RARE
WISDOM OF GOD IN EFFECTING THIS AS THE CURIOUS
WORKMANSHIP WITH WHICH THE CUP SHALL BE ENAMELED.

WILLIAM GURNALL

As Christians, we praise God for his marvelous grace in saving us—in setting his love on sinful people and then drawing them out of darkness and into life, out of the grave and into glory. But as William Gurnall tells us here, God displays his wisdom not only in the end, but also through the means. While for all eternity we will praise God *that* he saved us, we will also praise him for *how* he saved us. For what love but God's could have reached out to people who had blasphemed his name and declared him an enemy? What mind but God's could have conceived of a means to salvation that came by grace rather than works? What wisdom but God's could have understood that the one who bridges the infinite chasm between divinity and humanity must be both God and man? Who else would have been willing and able to send his very own Son into this world, to add a human nature to his divine nature, to live a perfect life, to die an atoning death, to take the sin of humanity upon his own shoulders, and to give them his own righteousness? Who else but our all-wise God?

NOT UNTIL WE HAVE
BECOME HUMBLE AND TEACHABLE,
STANDING IN AWE OF GOD'S
HOLINESS AND SOVEREIGNTY . . .
ACKNOWLEDGING OUR OWN LITTLENESS,
DISTRUSTING OUR OWN THOUGHTS,
& WILLING TO HAVE OUR MINDS
TURNED UPSIDE DOWN,
CAN DIVINE WISDOM
BECOME OURS.

J.I. PACKER

Though wisdom is an attribute of God, it is an attribute that is communicable—one that may be ours. But it may be ours only if we receive it from God's hand and on God's terms. It certainly cannot be conjured up from within and cannot be earned or deserved. It can only be called down from above, gracefully distributed by God himself. Wisdom comes to those who are humble and teachable, not to those who are proud and self-assured. Wisdom flows to those who know themselves to be "little" before God, those who have greater confidence in God's thoughts than in their own, who are willing and eager to think in divinely paradoxical ways rather than merely human ways. God makes wisdom available to those who long for it and who request it as a gift from his hand. "If any of you lacks wisdom, let him ask God, who gives generously to all without reproach, and it will be given him" (James 1:5). So ask in faith and expect to receive it.

The truly wise man is he who always believes the Bible against the opinion of any man.

R.A. Torrey

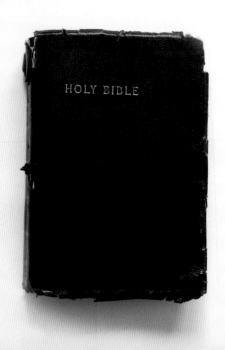

The all-wise God is the origin of all that counts as true wisdom. And this God has chosen to offer to each of us the fountain of wisdom by giving us his Word. If we wish to be wise as God is wise, if we wish to display his wisdom, we must look to his Word. We must read it, meditate upon it, understand it, obey it, and rightly apply it to the circumstances of our lives. We must choose to believe that in its pages we will learn who God is, we will learn who we most truly are, and we will learn what God requires of us. We must choose to believe that its wisdom is superior to any other source of wisdom and must allow it to reign supreme over the opinions and proclamations of any mere human being. As the Catechism says, "The word of God, which is contained in the scriptures of the Old and New Testaments, is the only rule to direct us how we may glorify and enjoy him." And because God has given us his Word, we have the great joy of honoring him by honoring it.

GOD IS
POWERFUL

You and I have power—we have abilities we can use to act in particular ways. We can speak, we can move, we can help or hinder, we can create or destroy. Yet it's abundantly clear that our abilities are limited. Few of us are good at more than a handful of things, and fewer of us still are the best at anything we do. The abilities we have are gained through hard practice, they can always be improved, and they inevitably begin to decline with age or disuse. Though we are powerful, we are only ever partially and imperfectly powerful.

This is not the way with God, for he is infinite, eternal, and unchangeable in his power. He has never had to learn any of his capabilities, has never had to practice them, and he is in no danger of ever seeing them decline. There is no other being that can counter his power and no place where his power is ineffective or even less effective. Thus, God is not merely powerful, but all-powerful and the source of every other power so that every act of every man, angel, or animal is permitted by his will and, in some way, under his hand. Let's use a collection of words from the wise to help us further consider the unsurpassed power of our great God.

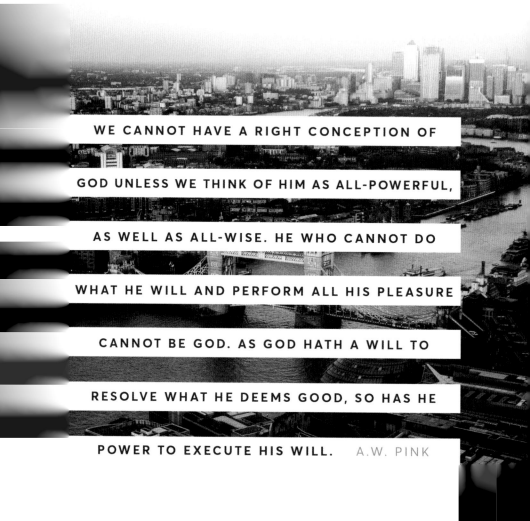

WE CANNOT HAVE A RIGHT CONCEPTION OF GOD UNLESS WE THINK OF HIM AS ALL-POWERFUL, AS WELL AS ALL-WISE. HE WHO CANNOT DO WHAT HE WILL AND PERFORM ALL HIS PLEASURE CANNOT BE GOD. AS GOD HATH A WILL TO RESOLVE WHAT HE DEEMS GOOD, SO HAS HE POWER TO EXECUTE HIS WILL. A.W. PINK

We have established that God is wise—that his perfect knowledge leads to perfect wisdom. Yet this is merely a partial description of God, for he is far more than that. As A.W. Pink tells us, "We cannot have a right conception of God unless we think of him as all-powerful, as well as all-wise." If God had the will to bring about the best results and if he had wisdom to know how to best accomplish his will, yet lacked the power to accomplish it, he could hardly be God. In fact, he would be little more than a human being, for we often have good desires and good plans, yet no ability to actually bring them about. For God to be worthy of our awe, worthy of our praise, worthy of our deepest devotion, he must have power that none can contain, interrupt, or diminish. For just as God has a will that is able to resolve and determine what he deems good, he also has the power to execute it—to ensure that his will is done on earth, as it is in heaven.

GOD IN HIS LOVE ALWAYS WILLS WHAT IS BEST FOR US. IN HIS WISDOM HE ALWAYS KNOWS WHAT IS BEST, AND IN HIS SOVEREIGNTY HE HAS THE POWER TO BRING IT ABOUT.

JERRY BRIDGES

God has wisdom to know what is best and wisdom to know how to accomplish it by the best possible means. And as we have learned, he also has power to execute it all. But we may wonder, as it pertains to us, what is his will? What does his wisdom determine is best? What is he accomplishing through the execution of his power? The book of Romans contains words of tremendous comfort: "And we know that for those who love God all things work together for good, for those who are called according to his purpose" (Romans 8:28). God's will is our good, which means that God's wisdom and power are directed at accomplishing what is ultimately for our good, and accomplishing it all in the best ways. All the things we experience, all the things we undergo, all the things we endure—all the things we celebrate and lament, the things that make us laugh and cry—all of them are born of God's love, directed at our good, and executed in the way that is nothing short of perfect.

The truth of God's **limitless power** would be absolutely terrifying were it not paired with the truth of **his limitless goodness.**

Jen Wilkin

No element of God's character can be separated from any other. You or I may use the power available to us recklessly, imperfectly, or sinfully—we may act forcefully yet unwisely, authoritatively yet with evil motives and immoral outcomes. We may act impulsively or on the basis of false information or in ways that foster prejudice or injustice. In this way, power can be used to bring about great good or great harm. But God never acts in such a way that he diminishes any part of his character. Hence, when God acts in power, he invariably exercises that power in ways that are wise, holy, just, good, and true. As Jen Wilkin tells us, God's power without his other attributes would be terrifying, for there would be nothing that would withhold or restrain him. Yet God's power paired with his other attributes is tremendously comforting, for we know he will use his power only in ways that are ultimately for our good and his glory.

THE POWER OF GOD IS THAT ABILITY AND

STRENGTH WHEREBY HE CAN BRING TO PASS

WHATSOEVER HE PLEASES, WHATSOEVER HIS

INFINITE WISDOM MAY DIRECT, AND WHATSOEVER

THE INFINITE PURITY OF HIS WILL MAY RESOLVE.

...

STEPHEN CHARNOCK

To have power is to have ability and strength. This is true whether the power belongs to human beings or to God himself—to creatures or to the Creator. Of course, our power is derived from God's, but his is inherent. We are accountable to God for the way we use our power, but God is accountable only to himself. Our power is always small and incomplete, but God's is always unbounded and unlimited. To say we are powerful is to say we possess the ability to do some of the things we desire some of the time. But to say God is powerful is to say God always possesses within himself the means necessary to bring about whatsoever he wills—to execute all his plans, to execute them all the way to perfect completion, and to overcome any and all resistance. This guarantees that God's will *will* be done, for as the psalmist says, "Our God is in the heavens; he does all that he pleases" (Psalm 115:3). Whatever his will resolves, however his wisdom directs, his power will accomplish.

The sovereignty of God is that golden scepter in his hand by which he will make all bow, either by <u>his word</u> or by <u>his works</u>, by <u>his mercies</u> or by <u>his judgments</u>.

THOMAS BENTON BROOKS

God is often described as being sovereign. "Sovereign" is a word of royalty or kingship that describes one who has supreme power and authority within his rightful jurisdiction—both the right and the ability to act in the ways he sees fit. A king has the right to act only within his own kingdom, yet because God created the world and owns it and fills it, his dominion extends through all time and all space—through all that is and all that will be. It extends even to each human being, for all have been created by God and all, therefore, owe allegiance to him. As sovereign, God has purposed to have all bow the knee to him, their rightful ruler. And through his power all will, though in different ways. Some will see his word and his works, respond to his mercy, and bow in worship. Some will see his word and works, harden their hearts, and be forced to bow before him in judgment. But either way, all *will* bow before him.

God does not do many things that he can,
but he does all things that he will.

George Swinnock

Theologians have long distinguished between what God can do and what God does do—between his absolute power and his ordained power.[4] God's absolute power is his ability to do whatever he pleases. There is no limit to what he can or could do. Hence, he could have created a second earth or several more moons. He could have created a world where the natural laws of gravity or relativity worked differently. He could have created a world without you or me. He could have wiped out humanity at the time of the Flood and been perfectly justified in doing so. He could have, but he did not. Hence, as Swinnock says, "God does not do many things that He can"—many things that he has the ability to do. This is his absolute power, and it must be distinguished from his ordained power—the power God has actually chosen to exercise. God exercises his power in such a way that "He does all things that He will." His power is such that he accomplishes all the things he desires and determines he will accomplish—with no man or woman, no force or creature, to hinder him or stand in his way.

*Before man can work he must have
both tools and materials, but God began
with nothing, and by his word alone
out of nothing made all things.
The intellect cannot grasp it.*

A.W. PINK

Creation communicates, for God has chosen to display something of himself through the things he has made. As the apostle Paul says, "his invisible attributes, namely, his eternal power and divine nature, have been clearly perceived, ever since the creation of the world, in the things that have been made" (Romans 1:20). There is much we can learn about God through the universe he has made, but primarily this: his eternal power and his divine nature. Those who gaze at the night skies, those who stand on the edge of the great canyons, those who gaze at the intricate perfection of a newborn baby, are looking at undeniable proof of God's existence and power. Paul goes on to say, "So they are without excuse." Because God has expressed himself through creation and given proof of his eternal power and divine nature, we are under obligation to believe—to admit that God is real and to submit ourselves to his power, his rule.

CAN THAT ALMIGHTY CREATOR, WHICH MADE ALL THINGS OF NOTHING, LACK MEANS TO BRING TO PASS IN HEAVEN AND EARTH WHATSOEVER HE PLEASES?

John Greene

There is a link between God's activity in creating the world and his activity in preserving the world—between his power displayed in creation and his power displayed in providence. Though there are some who imagine God as a kind of divine clockmaker who made the world, set it in motion according to natural laws and principles, and who then stepped back to allow it to operate on its own, the Bible presents God as being intricately involved in its smallest details. The one who made the world remains sovereign over the world and all that happens within it, so that "he does according to his will among the host of heaven and among the inhabitants of the earth; and none can stay his hand or say to him, 'What have you done?'" (Daniel 4:35). The God who was unrestrained in creating the world is the very same God who is unrestrained in bringing about his divine will within it, for he lacks nothing that would enable him to "bring to pass in heaven and earth whatsoever he pleases."

If there is one single molecule in this universe running around loose, totally free of God's sovereignty, then we have no guarantee that a single promise of God will ever be fulfilled.

R.C. Sproul

God's power is closely related to God's promises. In fact, God's unlimited power—his omnipotence—is inexorably connected to his promises, for if God does not have complete sovereignty, then the best we can do is hope that nothing will interfere with his good purposes and that nothing will interrupt his best promises. If there is as much as one rogue molecule in this universe—the smallest bit of matter that is not fully within the grip of God—then God's power is incomplete, and his rule is breakable. For it is possible that this one molecule will be the one that obstructs or impedes his plans. And if there is one rogue molecule, there is always the possibility of another and another. Thus, if we mean to take comfort in God's promises, if we mean to anchor our hope on them, we must first establish the fact that God is absolutely sovereign over every single thing and every single being, every single molecule and every single soul.

THE SOVEREIGNTY OF GOD IS OFTEN
QUESTIONED BECAUSE MAN DOES NOT
UNDERSTAND WHAT GOD IS DOING.
BECAUSE HE DOES NOT ACT AS WE THINK
HE SHOULD, WE CONCLUDE HE CANNOT
ACT AS WE THINK HE WOULD.

Jerry Bridges

We are often tempted to doubt that God is truly exercising his power in this world because we do not understand what he is doing. This is particularly true when we experience suffering and sorrow, pain and persecution. In such times we are prone to assume that God's power must have been diminished or superseded. After all, why would he cause or permit such painful circumstances to come upon us? But here the great poet William Cowper offers words of encouragement: "Judge not the Lord by feeble sense, / But trust Him for His grace; / Behind a frowning providence / He hides a smiling face." We must not judge God's character or works by our own feeble senses, but rather trust him—trust that his love for us is undiminished and his purposes for us undisturbed. By faith, we need to believe that behind the difficult providence is the smiling face of God, who is at work to bring good to his people and glory to his name. Though we may not be able to easily see it, by his grace we can and must believe it!

It is impossible for that man to despair who remembers that his Helper is omnipotent.

JEREMY TAYLOR

Knowing God and submitting our lives to his rule in no way guarantees a life of ease. This should be no surprise, for Jesus himself—who knew God, who submitted to God, and who *is* God—experienced all manner of suffering and sorrow. And he told those who would follow him, "If anyone would come after me, let him deny himself and take up his cross and follow me. For whoever would save his life will lose it, but whoever loses his life for my sake will find it" (Matthew 16:24-25). So when we do experience times of grief and loss, of trial and temptation, we need not despair. We need not despair because we know that God is not lacking in ability. He has the power to change our circumstances and to end our suffering, which means that if it continues, it must be within his will, it must be an exercise of his power, and it must be bringing about his good and perfect purposes. Thus, "It is impossible for that man to despair who remembers that his Helper is omnipotent."

SEEING THAT

HE IS CLOTHED

WITH OMNIPOTENCE,

NO PRAYER IS TOO HARD

FOR HIM TO ANSWER,

NO NEED TOO GREAT

FOR HIM TO SUPPLY,

NO PASSION TOO STRONG

FOR HIM TO SUBDUE;

NO TEMPTATION TOO POWERFUL

FOR HIM TO DELIVER FROM,

NO MISERY TOO DEEP

FOR HIM TO RELIEVE.

A.W. Pink

God's power has practical implications, including this: It makes it possible for us to pray to him with confidence and boldness. It would be folly to pray to a powerless deity—one whose intentions are good but who has no ability to bring them about. It would be discouraging to pray to a partially powerful God—one whose intentions are good but who can only bring about some of them some of the time. But there is nothing wiser than to pray to a powerful deity—one whose intentions are good and whose abilities know no bounds. So when we pray, we can be confident that "no prayer is too hard for Him to answer, no need too great for Him to supply, no passion too strong for Him to subdue; no temptation too powerful for Him to deliver from, no misery too deep for Him to relieve." We can bring all our fears, our sorrows, our griefs, our longings, our temptations, and our desires, and plead for his help, for his strength. We can ask with confidence that he *can* act, and with confidence that he *will* act.

GOD IS
HOLY

In the English language we have different ways of adding emphasis to certain words or of elevating them to superlatives. We may use words like "very" or "extremely" to differentiate between a person who is merely tall and one who is extraordinarily tall. We may add a suffix like "-est" to indicate that a person is not just tall, but tallest of all. The Hebrew language tended to accomplish this through repetition, and the great pastor-theologian R.C. Sproul was fond of pointing out that in all of Scripture, only one attribute of God was elevated to the third degree: God is often described as being holy, to be certain, but he is also described as being holy, holy, holy.

According to the Catechism, God is infinite, eternal, and unchangeable in his holiness. His holiness extends throughout all places so that there is no place where he is unholy. His holiness extends through all time so there is no occasion in the past in which he behaved in an unholy way, no occasion in the future in which he will act in a way that is less than perfectly holy. His holiness is unchangeable, so he can never cease being perfectly and wondrously holy. Let's take some time now to ponder our God, who is holy and even holy, holy, holy.

> *No other attribute is joined to the name of God* with greater frequency *than* holiness.

Jen Wilkin

A.W. Tozer famously said that "what comes into our minds when we think about God is the most important thing about us."[5] If this is true, then it is worth asking, what traits do you think of when you think about God? Do you think of his judgment? His wrath? His patience? His love? Here, Jen Wilkin reminds us of an important fact: There is no attribute that the Bible joins to God more frequently than his holiness. This means that when the people who authored the Bible considered God, and indeed when God considered God (since he, after all, is the ultimate author of Scripture), thoughts of his holiness were never far away. Neither has it even been far from the creatures who stand before him, for their cry is "Holy, holy, holy is the LORD of hosts; the whole earth is full of his glory!" (Isaiah 6:3). And so as much as we may prize God's other precious qualities, and as much as we may count them dear, we must never fail to consider that God is holy—and even holy, holy, holy—for as we have said, this attribute alone is raised to the superlative and beyond by its threefold repetition.

WHAT THEN
IS GOD'S HOLINESS?
WHAT DO WE MEAN WHEN WE
SAY "HOLY FATHER" & "HOLY SON"
& "HOLY SPIRIT" & "HOLY TRINITY"?
WE MEAN THE PERFECTLY PURE
DEVOTION OF EACH OF THESE
THREE PERSONS TO
THE OTHER TWO.

Sinclair Ferguson

The term "holiness" is often defined as "set apart," so that the holy objects in the Old Testament temple were the ones that were set apart for sacred ceremonies, and God's people were set apart from all other nations to be his own possession. Yet if God is holy in and of himself—holy without reference to anyone or anything he has made—there must be more to holiness than merely being set apart by him or for him. There must be a way of defining the term that doesn't focus on a distance from God or "set apartness" from God. It is perhaps then better to understand holiness as devotion to God. "What do we mean when we say 'Holy Father' and 'Holy Son' and 'Holy Spirit' and 'Holy Trinity'? We mean the perfectly pure devotion of each of these three persons to the other two." God's holiness, then, refers primarily to God's devotion to God—his undivided and perfectly pure love, loyalty, enthusiasm, and commitment for himself. This is a love that flows first within the persons of the Trinity and only later extends beyond God to the creatures he has made.

*An ineffably holy God, who has the utmost abhorrence of all sin,
was never invented by any of Adam's fallen descendants.*

A.W. PINK

There are many reasons to believe in God, many ways we can know he exists, and many reasons to believe that the God of the Bible is the one true, living God. Here is a particularly interesting one: No human being would invent a God who is ineffably holy—holy above and beyond all we can imagine, all we can explain, all we can comprehend. And no human being would invent a God who, in his holiness, has a complete and utter abhorrence of all sin. We may invent a God who dislikes sin and demands we do good to balance it out; we may invent a God who dislikes sin and chooses to shrug it off; but surely we would never invent a God whose very nature is opposed to sin and who responds to it with wrathful revulsion. For to invent such a God would be to invent one who is opposed to our very selves since we, after all, are so clearly and undeniably sinful. In that way, the holiness of God is proof of God—proof of his sheer otherness from all that is.

AS GOD'S POWER IS THE
OPPOSITE OF THE NATIVE
WEAKNESS OF THE CREATURE,
AS HIS WISDOM IS IN COMPLETE
CONTRAST FROM THE LEAST
DEFECT OF UNDERSTANDING OR
FOLLY, SO HIS HOLINESS IS THE
VERY ANTITHESIS OF ALL MORAL
BLEMISH OR DEFILEMENT.

A.W. PINK

Sometimes we can best understand a quality by its opposites: We understand darkness to be opposed to light, sorrow to be opposed to joy, death to be opposed to life. And this is how A.W. Pink approaches the matter of holiness: He shows how holiness is the absence of the all-too-familiar negative qualities associated with our fallen humanity. He tells us that just as God's power is the opposite of our weakness and God's wisdom is the opposite of our folly, God's holiness is the opposite of our sin—the opposite of our moral blemishes and ethical defilements. To admit that we are sinners, to admit that we are deeply morally flawed, to admit that we have defiled ourselves and our relationship to God through our lack of perfection, is to admit that we are not holy. For holiness is the antithesis of blemishes, the antithesis of defilement, a complete and total contrast from all that is sin and sinful.

A true love of God must begin with a delight in his holiness, and not with a delight in any other attribute;

for no other attribute is truly lovely without this.

JONATHAN EDWARDS

There are many reasons we ought to love God. We ought to love him for all that he is and for all that he has done. Those lists alone would stretch into infinity. Yet here Jonathan Edwards suggests that we ought to love God foremost for his holiness, that for all we love about God, this should be at the very top. Why? Because God's holiness touches all his other attributes in such a way as to make them delightful. If God was powerful but not holy, he might misuse his power to bring about evil ends instead of good ones, and he might misuse his authority to promote what is ultimately to our harm instead of to our good. If God was just but not holy, he might be arbitrary and capricious, a judge who makes poor judgments or who shows favoritism and partiality. But because God is holy, we can have complete confidence that every one of his attributes is holy and that every one of his acts is holy—completely pure, completely distinct from any kind of sin or weakness, and completely devoted to his purposes. We can have total confidence in him.

Holiness in angels
and saints is but a
quality, but in God
it is his essence.

THOMAS BROOKS

God is holy, but he is not alone in being holy. The angels, those servants who dwell in his presence and do his bidding, are holy, for Jesus says, "For whoever is ashamed of me and of my words, of him will the Son of Man be ashamed when he comes in his glory and the glory of the Father and of the holy angels" (Luke 9:26). Likewise, we who are saved by his gospel are declared holy and then instructed to become increasingly holy: "It is written, 'You shall be holy, for I am holy'" (1 Peter 1:16). But there is an important distinction between the holiness of God and the holiness of men or angels: "Holiness in angels and saints is but a quality, but in God it is his essence." We are holy only because God has communicated this attribute to us. It is something that is given or conveyed, not something that is part of our very essence. Hence where it is possible for there to be unholy humans and fallen angels, it is impossible for there to be an unholy God. For without his holiness, God could not be God.

No attribute of God is more dreadful to sinners than his holiness.

MATTHEW HENRY

Many people scorn the God of the Bible and replace him with a God of their own imagining. Yet, as we have seen, no one would invent a God who is holy, much less holy, holy, holy—holy to the most superlative degree. No sinner would invent such a God because his holiness is the attribute they dread and despise the most, for if God is holy, he expects us to be holy. If God is without blemish, he expects us to be without blemish. If God is completely devoted to his own purposes, he expects we will also be completely devoted to his own purposes. To admit God's holiness is to admit our own depravity and how far we fall short of his glory. To admit how far we fall short of his glory is to admit how deserving we are of his censure and his condemnation. Hence, this attribute can only generate dread and denial in the hearts of those who have chosen to live for their purposes and according to their own law.

If you don't delight in the fact that your Father is holy, holy, holy, then you are spiritually dead. You may be in a church. You may go to a Christian school. But if there is no delight in your soul for the holiness of God, you don't know God. You don't love God. You're out of touch with God. You're asleep to his character. R.C. Sproul

If the holiness of God is dreadful to those who hate him, it is delightful to those who love him. As God calls us to himself and increasingly reveals himself to our spiritual sight, we come to see him as perfectly and transcendently holy. This is meant to stir up a great love, awe, and respect for him. And here R.C. Sproul offers a solemn warning: "If there is no delight in your soul for the holiness of God, you don't know God. You don't love God." Why is this? Because those who do not know God as holy don't know God as he really is. Such people are worshipping a God who is different from the one who reveals himself in the world around and in the pages of holy Scripture. They are out of touch with God and asleep to the most precious qualities of his character, in denial of his most essential attributes. With spiritual life comes an appreciation of God's holiness and a longing to display it in our own hearts, our own minds, our own lives—to be holy even as God is holy.

THERE IS A

DANGER OF FORGETTING

THAT THE BIBLE REVEALS, NOT

FIRST THE LOVE OF GOD, BUT THE

INTENSE, BLAZING HOLINESS

OF GOD, WITH HIS LOVE AS

THE CENTER OF THAT

HOLINESS.

Oswald Chambers

We love the love of God, and well we should. God's love is precious and wonderful and is all that stands between us and the punishment we so richly deserve. And because we can never exhaust the love of God, we must never cease worshipping God for his love. Yet we need to ensure that we do not separate God's love from his holiness, for the two are inexorably connected. As Chambers says, before God reveals himself as loving, he reveals himself as holy. We cannot understand the character of God's love, nor its depths, until we understand his holiness. For it is when we see God in his holiness and ourselves in our depravity that we come to understand the true magnitude of his love. Our sin is not a minor detail that God chooses to overlook, but a problem of the greatest extent, a defiance of the deepest kind. And yet this holy, holy, holy God made a way where we could not only be reconciled to him but also be made holy like him.

IF GOD IS HOLY,
THEN HE CAN'T SIN.
IF GOD CAN'T SIN, THEN
HE CAN'T SIN AGAINST ME.
IF HE CAN'T SIN AGAINST ME,
SHOULDN'T THAT MAKE HIM
THE MOST TRUSTWORTHY
BEING THERE IS?

Jackie Hill Perry

God's holiness is not an abstract quality or one that is completely disconnected from our relationship with him. No, it is a practical quality that changes the very nature of the way we relate to him. Jackie Hill Perry's step-by-step explanation is clarifying: "If God is holy, then he can't sin. If God can't sin, then he can't sin against me. If he can't sin against me, shouldn't that make him the most trustworthy being there is?" Indeed, it should. When we trust that God cannot sin—and further, cannot make any mistakes and cannot do anything less than what is best—we can have great confidence that he cannot sin against us and cannot do anything other than what is good and what is best. And if all this is true, it makes him a being who is eminently trustworthy, eminently worthy of our highest confidence. An unholy God would be unworthy of our love and unworthy of our trust, but a holy God is worthy of our fullest love and highest confidence, for he will only ever do what is best, what is for his greatest glory and our highest good.

Satan knows well the power of

TRUE HOLINESS

and the immense injury which

INCREASED ATTENTION

to it will do to his kingdom.

J.C. RYLE

We are called to God so we can become holy like God. He means for us to be as devoted to his purposes as he is and for that reason begins to transform us from the inside out—from the mind and heart to the hands and mouth. Yet every Christian can attest that it is difficult to put sin to death and to come alive to righteousness. Every Christian can attest that we meet resistance on every side. And little wonder, for Satan is the great enemy of God and therefore the great enemy of holiness. "We do not wrestle against flesh and blood, but against the rulers, against the authorities, against the cosmic powers over this present darkness, against the spiritual forces of evil in the heavenly places" (Ephesians 6:12). We must stand firm in the power God provides, resisting the enemy of our souls. Satan knows that Christians living holy lives—living out God's own holiness—would damage his cause in the world. Hence, he battles hard to tempt us, to draw us away from God's purposes and toward his own.

TO BE HOLY,
TO BE SANCTIFIED,
THEREFORE,
TO BE A "SAINT,"
IS IN SIMPLE TERMS
TO BE DEVOTED
TO GOD.

SINCLAIR FERGUSON

God's holiness is his devotion to himself—the devotion of each person of the Godhead to the other two. Yet God's holiness is not an attribute that is found only within God, but one that is meant to be found also in the people he saves to himself. And it is when we understand God's devotion to himself that we unlock the key to the holiness he requires from us. "To be holy, to be sanctified, therefore, to be a 'saint,' is in simple terms to be devoted to God." The term "sanctified" refers to this lifelong process of becoming holy so that our every desire, our every thought, our every word, and our every deed is devoted to God, consistent with what he expects of us and what he requires from us. Those of us who have responded to the gospel by faith are now saints, people who are set apart to be fully devoted to the one who has so freely and graciously proven his devotion to us.

GOD IS
JUST

We all have a longing for justice. Every human being wishes to see good deeds rewarded and evil deeds punished according to a standard of justice. In other words, every human being wishes to see people treated in the way they deserve. The difficulty, of course, is that we cannot agree among ourselves on a universal standard of good and evil and, therefore, on a universal system of justice. The Catechism tells us that God is infinite, eternal, and unchangeable in his justice. He was perfectly just before the world began and the first act of injustice was committed. He will remain just long after this world has ceased to be. His standard of justice has never changed, but is the same yesterday, today, and forever. His unchanging standard of justice extends over every people, every nation, every tribe and tongue that ever has existed or ever will exist. In other words, God himself is the very standard of justice, the one from whom all true justice flows. If we wish to know what constitutes justice, and if we wish to learn how to live upright, honorable, and just lives, we must look to him. Let's consider together the God who is completely and perfectly just.

By justice is meant that rectitude of character which leads to the treatment of others in strict accordance with their deserts.

———————————

J.P. BOYCE

God is infinite, eternal, and unchangeable in his justice. Justice is a term we hear and use often today and one to which we assign a variety of meanings. But when applied to God, it refers to a quality of his character that is displayed in the way he treats others. His justice is his perfect uprightness, his correct moral thinking and judgment. He possesses this in and of himself, without reference to any other creature, so that before God created anyone or anything, he was perfectly just. But as the Creator, God now exercises his justice in such a way that it causes him to treat others exactly the way they deserve.[6] As the one who is perfectly just, he has created a law and now judges his creatures according to their adherence to it. Those who have held perfectly to the law are judged perfect by God; those who have violated the law in any of its parts are judged guilty by God. Either way, God treats others in precisely the way they deserve, without bias, without partiality, without incomplete knowledge, and without error.

THE JUDGE OF ALL THE EARTH MUST DO RIGHT.
THEREFORE IT WAS IMPOSSIBLE BY THE
NECESSITIES OF HIS OWN BEING THAT

---

he should deal lightly with sin, and
compromise the claims of holiness.

Harold Guillebaud

If God is perfectly just, it is impossible for him to fail to dispense justice. Having created a law that was consistent with his character, a law that provided the moral code for the entire creation, it would be morally abhorrent for God to fail to uphold the demands of the law— to fail to judge innocent those who have upheld the law and to judge guilty those who have not. This means he could not simply shrug off sin or deal with it lightly. He could not fail to judge those who rebelled against the law and chose to live according to a law of their own. For God to be just, he must see that justice is done. The quote from Guillebaud continues with this: "If sin could be forgiven at all, it must be on the basis which would vindicate the holy law of God." If there was to be forgiveness for sin, it must come in a way that would not violate the law, but rather vindicate it. And so we naturally wonder, could there be such a way?

AT THE CROSS, IN HOLY LOVE,

GOD, THROUGH CHRIST, PAID THE FULL

PENALTY OF OUR DISOBEDIENCE HIMSELF.

HE BORE THE JUDGMENT WE DESERVE IN ORDER

TO BRING US THE FORGIVENESS WE DO NOT

DESERVE. ON THE CROSS DIVINE MERCY AND

JUSTICE WERE EQUALLY EXPRESSED AND

ETERNALLY RECONCILED. GOD'S HOLY

LOVE WAS "SATISFIED."

JOHN STOTT

Could there be a way that God would be both perfectly holy and perfectly just? Could he extend mercy while still maintaining justice? God made a way! John Stott says, "At the cross, in holy love, God, through Christ, paid the full penalty of our disobedience Himself." To our great amazement, we learn that God did not only dispense justice but also received it! The God who demanded payment also made the payment. Stott continues: "He bore the judgment we deserve in order to bring us the forgiveness we do not deserve." Something unimaginably wonderful transpired in the death of Jesus Christ: "On the cross divine mercy and justice were equally expressed and eternally reconciled. God's holy love was 'satisfied.'" At the cross, the pure and perfect God the Son faced the holy wrath of the pure and perfect God the Father so that mercy and justice were both expressed and reconciled on our behalf. What wondrous love is this!

The wonder of the cross is that in the very same stroke it satisfies **both** the love of God and the justice of God.

— TIMOTHY KELLER

We tend to set certain characteristics at odds with one another, as if to exemplify one virtue means it is impossible to exemplify a second. This is exactly the case when it comes to love and justice, for we tend to think that those who have committed deeds of great evil can receive either love or justice, but not both. We must choose between expressing love by overlooking their offense or expressing justice by making them atone for it. But God is not so limited, and he knew a way to express both the highest love and the truest justice. "The wonder of the cross is that in the very same stroke it satisfies both the love of God and the justice of God." God expresses his love in saving sinners from the just consequences of their sin, yet at the very same time and in the very same act he expresses his justice in saving sinners by his love. He does this by substitution, by crediting our sin to Jesus, who paid the cost, and by crediting Christ's righteousness to us. What a wonder, indeed!

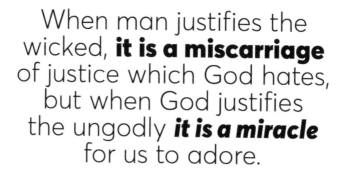

When man justifies the wicked, **it is a miscarriage** of justice which God hates, but when God justifies the ungodly ***it is a miracle*** for us to adore.

J.I. PACKER

The key to this quote is understanding two different uses of "justify." When a human being justifies a person who has behaved in a way that is sinful, it is a miscarriage of justice. For in this use of the word, the person has simply chosen to overlook a person's sin or crime, to act as if it didn't happen. This fails to give justice to the person who has been wronged. A man whose possessions have been stolen or a wife whose husband has been murdered is wronged when the thief or murderer is let off without consequences. But when God justifies the ungodly, he does so on the basis of consequences meted out and fully paid. The sins of the one who has been justified were placed on Jesus Christ, who took them upon himself and fully paid the cost for them in the sight of God. In that way, the debt has been paid, the account has been settled, and the offender can rightly be declared fully righteous.

The Scriptures find the justice of God a virtue to be extolled, *not* a blemish to be concealed.

Jen Wilkin

There are some who are ashamed of God's justice and his demand that the guilty be judged guilty. Others minimize this attribute as if it were a divine blemish or awkward embarrassment that would be better to conceal. Yet the Bible praises God for his justice and extols him for his righteousness. "But the LORD sits enthroned forever; he has established his throne for justice, and he judges the world with righteousness; he judges the peoples with uprightness" (Psalm 9:7-8). How does David respond to this? "I will give thanks to the LORD with my whole heart; I will recount all of your wonderful deeds. I will be glad and exult in you; I will sing praise to your name, O Most High" (Psalm 9:1-2). None of us truly wishes to live in a world marked by injustice and unrighteousness. And because justice and righteousness are found in God and flow from him, we do not have to! The justice we crave is first the justice that flows from the heart of a God who is just and who must see justice prevail.

Don't ever ask God for justice —you might get it.

R.C. SPROUL

We have a natural longing for justice—a natural longing for good to be rewarded and for evil to be punished. Yet as R.C. Sproul soberly warns us here, we need to be careful what we wish for. If we are to demand justice when others offend us, we are at the same time demanding justice for our offenses against them and against God. We cannot have it both ways and cannot wish to live in a world of partial justice—a world in which we get away with our sins while others are punished for theirs. If we are to seek justice, we must seek it for all mankind, including ourselves. This is not to say, however, that we should be content with injustice! To the contrary, we should pray to God for justice to be done. But we should do more than this. We must take refuge in Christ, who has faced the Father's wrath against sin and withstood the full fury of his justice. When we come to Christ, all that is ours becomes his, and all that is his becomes ours. We do get justice after all—the justice of God as won by Christ.

A GOD WHO COULD PARDON WITHOUT JUSTICE

might one of these days condemn without reason.

Charles Spurgeon

Those who long for God to simply pardon sinners without ensuring justice has been done need to consider the implications of their desire. They need to consider what it would mean for God to simply overlook sins without upholding his standard of justice. Charles Spurgeon lays down the challenge when he points out that "a God who could pardon without justice might one of these days condemn without reason." If God were to let people get away with the least sin, he would show an inconsistency of character and show that he would at times be willing to bend the rules that govern his own domain. So even though this might permit him to pardon someone apart from justice, it might then also permit him to condemn someone apart from any evil deed. If he were to act arbitrarily in one direction, he might act arbitrarily in another. It is far better for God to be consistently just. And we have no need to fear his justice, for he has told us to flee by faith to Christ, who has already settled justice's demands on our behalf.

None are ruined by the justice of God *but those* that hate to be reformed by the grace of God.

Matthew Henry

The God who is just must see that justice is done—that each person is judged by the divine standard of righteousness. And indeed, all will stand before his judgment throne in that day when "each of us will give an account of himself to God" (Romans 14:12). But God has revealed the standard of his justice he will use. He has given us a great display of his love in the cross and has shown the way through which we can receive his mercy. In other words, he has made an offer of grace—of unmerited mercy—that extends to all of humanity. This means that those who face the full and final justice of God are only those who have rejected his free offer. As Matthew Henry says, "None are ruined by the justice of God but those that hate to be reformed by the grace of God." It is not God's wish that any should perish, but that all should be covered by the justice accomplished by Jesus Christ. It is only those who refuse who will, in the end, be "ruined" as they face his justice.

WHEN GOD'S JUSTICE FALLS, WE ARE OFFENDED BECAUSE WE THINK GOD OWES PERPETUAL MERCY. WE MUST NOT TAKE HIS GRACE FOR GRANTED. WE MUST NEVER LOSE OUR CAPACITY TO BE AMAZED BY HIS GRACE.

R.C. Sproul

The sun always looks brighter when it bursts through the clouds near the end of a rainy day. A diamond always seems to glitter with greater purity when it is held up against a dark backdrop. And what R.C. Sproul means for us to consider here is that the gospel of Jesus Christ is only seen to be wonderful when we understand it in the context of our sinfulness and God's demand for justice. When we believe God only ever dispenses mercy or perhaps that he even owes us mercy, the wonder of the gospel seems to decline. But when we believe that God always dispenses justice and that he even owes us justice, the wonder of the gospel must increase, for now we see mercy as a precious gift. We can be amazed by God's grace only when we see it set against the dark backdrop of our sin and within the context of God's perfect justice. When we find ourselves feeling humdrum about the gospel, perhaps it is because we have failed to consider justice.

MAY WE SIT AT
THE FOOT OF THE CROSS
AND THERE LEARN WHAT SIN
HAS DONE, WHAT JUSTICE
HAS DONE, WHAT LOVE
HAS DONE.

John Newton

The Christian life is a life that revolves around the cross of Christ. And while we can obviously not be physically present at the cross, we can always be spiritually present there by the means of grace God has provided. When we read Scripture and meditate upon it and when we participate in the ordinances of the Lord's Supper and baptism, we are able to "sit at the foot of the cross" by faith. And as we do that, as we ponder the suffering of our Lord and Savior Jesus Christ, we will learn what our sin has done. As we ponder the Father pouring out his just wrath upon Christ, we will learn what justice has done. As we ponder the perfection of Christ and consider that he is suffering for our sin rather than his own, when we consider the Son's cry of "My God, my God, why have you forsaken me?" we will learn what love has done. May each of us diligently sit at the foot of the cross to learn, to remember, to weep, and to worship.

GOD IS NOT ALWAYS A GOD OF IMMEDIATE JUSTICE, BUT HE IS A GOD OF ULTIMATE JUSTICE.

JOHN BLANCHARD

Though we long for justice, we do not always see it here and now. The Bible deals honestly with our longing and confusion: "Righteous are you, O Lord, when I complain to you; yet I would plead my case before you. Why does the way of the wicked prosper? Why do all who are treacherous thrive?" (Jeremiah 12:1). Yet perhaps the old saying is wrong that "justice delayed is justice denied." In his wisdom, God sometimes delays and sometimes withholds his hand for a time. John Blanchard assures us that though "God is not always a God of immediate justice . . . he is a God of ultimate justice." God sometimes stays his hand of judgment for a time when it is consistent with his purposes to do so. Yet he assures us that this is a temporary and not permanent state of affairs, for he will most certainly dispense ultimate judgment so that not the least sin is overlooked, and not the least virtuous deed unrewarded.

When we consider the character and attributes of our God, our thoughts tend to settle immediately on his love. And for good reason: "God is love" (1 John 4:16) and most profoundly "shows his love for us in that while we were still sinners, Christ died for us" (Romans 5:8). We love the love of God, for it is all that stands between us and an eternity of being cast out of his presence. Many inquisitive students have wondered why the theologians who wrote the Catechism did not include God's love in this list of attributes. While it is a valid question, the reason is actually very simple: Love is included within the more expansive attribute of goodness. Goodness includes love and also extends to related characteristics like mercy and patience. Thus, God is infinite, eternal, and unchangeable in his goodness, which means he is also infinite, eternal, and unchangeable in his love. From before eternity he was good, and into the distant reaches of time and space he will remain good—untainted by the least trace of evil. Let's turn to words from the wise to consider God's goodness and, with them and David, have our hearts moved to cry out "Oh give thanks to the LORD, for he is good; for his steadfast love endures forever!" (1 Chronicles 16:34).

GOD ONLY IS IMMUTABLY GOOD.

OTHER THINGS MAY BE PERPETUALLY GOOD

BY SUPERNATURAL POWER, BUT NOT

IMMUTABLY GOOD IN THEIR OWN NATURE.

OTHER THINGS ARE NOT SO GOOD,

BUT THEY MAY BE BAD; GOD IS SO GOOD

THAT HE CANNOT BE BAD.

STEPHEN CHARNOCK

God is a Spirit, infinite, eternal, and unchangeable in his goodness. Charnock uses the term "immutable" to refer to the fact that God is not only unchanging from age to age, but unchangeable. It is simply not possible for God to change in any attribute, including his goodness. And here he points to an important distinction between God's goodness and the goodness of any other creature. While other creatures, including human beings, may be good, that goodness is not inherent to their nature, but derived from God. And not only that, but that goodness is not immutable, which means it can be changed. Hence while humans are not so good that we can never behave badly, God is so good that it is impossible for him to ever be the least bit bad—to think badly, desire bad things, or to exercise his power toward bad outcomes. All that he is, all that he desires, all that he thinks, and all that he does is perfectly good, utterly without the least blemish.

What is "good?"
"Good" is what God approves.
We may ask then,
why is what God approves good?
We must answer,
"Because he approves it."
That is to say, there is no higher
standard of goodness than
God's own character and
his approval of whatever
is consistent with
that character.

Wayne Grudem

How can we know what is good? The answer is surprisingly simple: "Good" is what God approves—what he deems satisfactory according to his unchanging and unchangeable standard. Why are these things good? We are right back to where we began—these things are good because God approves them. As the very source of all that is good, he is the one who defines goodness. There is no higher standard that he must appeal to and no higher authority that he is accountable to. As Grudem says, "There is no higher standard of goodness than God's own character and His approval of whatever is consistent with that character." The question then follows: How can we know what is good? We would not know what is good or evil unless God had revealed it to us. Thankfully, by his grace, he has done this. In the words of the Bible, he has described his character, he has shown how this character manifests itself in interactions with others, and he has given us a law that is consistent with it. We can know what is good if we look to what God has revealed.

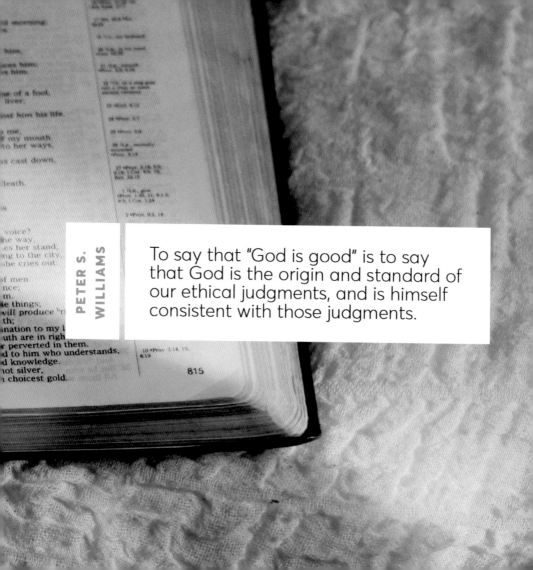

PETER S. WILLIAMS

To say that "God is good" is to say that God is the origin and standard of our ethical judgments, and is himself consistent with those judgments.

When we say "God is good," we are not simply stating an abstract fact, but also making a statement that has profound moral and ethical consequences. God's goodness is not merely a description of his nature, but also the basis of all his acts and all his judgments. Because God's nature is good, because his judgments are good, and because all his acts are good, there is an onus on us to make ethical judgments and to act on the basis of ethical standards. We must learn what our God deems to be good and then faithfully imitate him in his goodness. We cannot rightly declare "God is good" and then live in ways that are depraved and dissolute. To the contrary, when we declare "God is good," it calls us to live according to his goodness and to behave in such a way that we make his goodness known to others. When we know that our God is good, we know what he expects of us, and when we know what he expects of us, we delight to do it.

The goodness of God
is as curious as his
disappointments.

J.A. MOTYER

If God is truly God, if he is truly infinite, eternal, and unchangeable, and if he is working all things for his own glory rather than our comfort, we should not be surprised if at times we do not understand his acts. We should not be surprised if sometimes what he deems good does not immediately appear good to us. After all, we are finite, we are mortal, we are in a state of constant change, constant flux, constant adaptation to providence and circumstance. We have limited vision, limited knowledge, limited wisdom, limited power. This being the case, God's goodness is sometimes manifested in ways that perplex us, that disturb us, that even cause us to weep and grieve. Yet the faith that saves us is the same faith that calls us to trust him, even when his goodness "is as curious as his disappointments." In such times, we can and must make this our statement of faith and our petition: "You are good and do good. Teach me your statutes" (Psalm 119:68).

LOVE IS THE ONLY
ATTRIBUTE WHICH GOD
HATH ACTED TO THE UTMOST.
WE HAVE NEVER SEEN THE
UTMOST OF HIS POWER, WHAT
GOD CAN DO, BUT WE HAVE
SEEN THE UTMOST OF HIS
LOVE: HE HATH FOUND A
RANSOM FOR LOST SOULS.

Matthew Mead

As we read the Bible, as we enjoy God's creation, as we witness God's providence in the history of humanity, we see God acting in ways consistent with his attributes. We see many acts of wisdom, power, holiness, justice, goodness, and truth. And yet, as Matthew Mead expresses here, there is only one of his attributes that we see expressed in its fullest form, and that is his goodness as manifested in his love. We have never seen God act in the fullness of his power. We have never seen God express justice in its fullest form. We have never seen the total expression of God's holiness—and neither could we, since we simply could not withstand it. Yet we *have* seen the fullest possible expression of God's love, for never has it been, and never can it be, more fully and perfectly expressed than in his act of redeeming sinners to himself. There could be no greater expression of his love than the one we see in sacrificing his own Son to save sinners to himself. This is love at its utmost, love at its fullest form.

GOD'S LOVE
IS NOT DRAWN OUT BY OUR
LOVABLENESS, BUT WELLS UP,
LIKE AN ARTESIAN SPRING,
FROM THE DEPTHS OF
HIS NATURE.

Alexander
Maclaren

God makes it perfectly clear that he loves his people. Yet it is also perfectly clear that God does not love his people because of some innate lovableness—by being worthy of his love. God's love is not something that is owed to us because of any intrinsic goodness or loveliness that abides within us. Rather, God loves us because he is so very good, so very loving. The source of his love for us is not within us but within himself where, in the descriptive words of Alexander Maclaren, it "wells up, like an artesian spring, from the depths of his nature." As clear and pure water bubbles up from springs deep beneath the surface of the earth, clear and pure love wells up from within God's very nature. And he so graciously extends this love to us, even though we are undeserving, even though we are naturally unloving and unlovable. "See what kind of love the Father has given to us, that we should be called children of God; and so we are" (1 John 3:1).

There is no human wreckage, lying in the ooze of the deepest sea of iniquity, that God's deep love cannot reach & redeem.

JOHN HENRY JOWETT

Knowing our unlovable nature—aware of our sin, our depravity, our acts of rebellion against the Creator—we may wonder if we are beyond the love of God. We all sometimes fear that we have sinned beyond his capacity to forgive, that we have become depraved beyond his ability to redeem. This is where John Henry Jowett's words offer sweet comfort: "There is no human wreckage, lying in the ooze of the deepest sea of iniquity, that God's deep love cannot reach and redeem." He can offer these words with confidence because God's invitation goes out to all, with no qualification, no concern that its power is too small for those who have sinned so much. "Come to me, all who labor and are heavy laden, and I will give you rest" (Matthew 11:28). Jesus invites *all* who labor under the heavy weight of sin and iniquity, and he promises he *will* give them the rest of forgiveness. His power is vast, his arm is strong, his promise is reliable. None of us is beyond the reach of his love.

IF YOU DON'T THINK GOD'S LOVE FOR THE UNLOVABLE IS AMAZING, GO TRY TO LOVE SOMEONE WHO HATES YOU FOR A DAY. SEE IF THAT HELPS. KB

Because we speak so often and so freely of God's love, we need to guard ourselves against apathy, for as the old saying goes, familiarity breeds contempt. Even something as awe-inspiring as God's love for the lost can become so familiar that it begins to lose its wonder. And it is here that musician KB offers a challenge: "If you don't think God's love for the unlovable is amazing, go try to love someone who hates you for a day. See if that helps." And indeed, an honest assessment will show that we have trouble enough loving the people who love us over the course of an entire day, never mind the people who hate us, despise us, and actively seek to harm us. Yet when God says, "Love your enemies, do good to those who hate you, bless those who curse you, pray for those who abuse you" (Luke 6:27-28), he is asking us to do no more than he himself has done. We are never more fully imitating God's goodness than when we are extending love to those who consider us their enemies, for this is what God has done in drawing us to himself.

THE FACT
THAT YOU ARE
CURRENTLY INHALING
AND EXHALING AT THIS VERY
MOMENT MEANS THAT YOU
ARE A RECIPIENT
OF MERCY.

Jen Wilkin

As God's goodness is displayed in his love, it is also displayed in his mercy. If grace is God's favor toward those who are undeserving, mercy is his favor toward those who are incapable—those who have a desperate need they cannot meet in and of themselves. God's mercy is displayed at every moment of our lives and in the simplest of acts—even in the act of inhaling and exhaling at this very moment. For God could have justly struck us down at any time. He could have expressed his justice in sending us to hell in the moment of our first sin, or our last. But in his mercy he has allowed us to live on, to enjoy the beautiful things of this world, to enjoy the pleasures of this life. We continue to exist by his mercy and at every moment are the beneficiaries of it. "Give thanks to the LORD, for he is good, for his steadfast love endures forever" (Psalm 136:1)!

How slow God is to anger.
He was longer in destroying Jericho
than in making the world.

THOMAS WATSON

There are many ways in which God displays his mercy, and in this quote, Thomas Watson highlights an especially precious one: his patience. When God created Adam and Eve, he told them that rebellion against his rule would lead to the direst consequence: "You shall surely die" (Genesis 2:17). When they committed that rebellion, God told them they would indeed die and return to the ground: "For out of it you were taken; for you are dust, and to dust you shall return" (Genesis 3:19). However, instead of acting immediately, he held off the sentence until they had repented of their sin and lived long and fruitful lives. That was the first time God showed patience, but certainly not the last. Since that day, God has often revealed himself to his people as he did to Moses: "The Lord, the Lord, a God merciful and gracious, slow to anger, and abounding in steadfast love and faithfulness, keeping steadfast love for thousands, forgiving iniquity and transgression and sin" (Exodus 34:6-7). God shows his goodness in his mercy, and he shows his mercy in his patience.

FOR GOD TO BESTOW THE MERCY OF MERCIES,
THE MOST PRECIOUS THING IN HEAVEN OR EARTH,
UPON POOR SINNERS, AND AS GREAT, AS LOVELY,
AS EXCELLENT AS HIS SON WAS, YET NOT TO
ACCOUNT HIM TOO GOOD TO BESTOW UPON US,
WHAT MANNER OF LOVE IS THIS!

John Flavel

God displays his mercy in the smallest providences and simplest pleasures of this life. There is nothing we receive, nothing we enjoy, that is not a gift of his mercy. But God shows his mercy most vividly and most extravagantly in the greatest and most wonderful event in all of history—the atoning sacrifice of his Son. God has not merely bestowed upon us what was of little importance or little worth, but what was precious beyond all imagining and valuable above all reckoning. There was nothing in all of earth and heaven that was more valuable to God than his own Son, yet he did not count this too great or too costly a gift. "What manner of love is this!" exclaims John Flavel with awe, with wonder, with worship. What manner of love is this, that created beings bankrupted by our depravity have been given a divine gift of inestimable worth? Who but God would bestow upon us the very mercy of mercies, the very Son of God, to save us from our sin?

All the compassions *of all the tender fathers*
in the world compared with *the tender mercies of our God*
would be but as a candle *to the sun or a drop to the ocean.*

MATTHEW HENRY

We refer to the first person of the Trinity as "God the Father," and it is important to understand that God's fatherhood comes before any fatherhood among human beings. In other words, God did not create human fathers and then begin to describe himself in reference to them. Rather, God has always been Father and created human fathers in reference to him. Thus, when our earthly fathers act in compassion toward their children, they are merely imitating the compassion of the heavenly Father. "As a father shows compassion to his children, so the LORD shows compassion to those who fear him. For he knows our frame; he remembers that we are dust" (Psalm 103:13-14). Yet only God is infinitely, eternally, and unchangeably compassionate, which is why Matthew Henry can say that "all the compassions of all the tender fathers in the world compared with the tender mercies of our God would be but as a candle to the sun or a drop to the ocean." Even at our finest moment, we are only ever the palest imitations of the perfectly and wondrously compassionate God.

I HAVE BEEN A MAN OF GREAT
SINS, BUT HE HAS BEEN A GOD
OF GREAT MERCIES, AND NOW,
THROUGH HIS MERCIES, I HAVE
A CONSCIENCE AS SOUND
AND QUIET AS IF I HAD
NEVER SINNED.

Donald Cargill

We may become good at forgiving, but we are rarely good at forgetting. We may choose to express mercy to others, but we often still dwell upon the wrongs that have been done to us. But when God expresses the mercy of forgiveness, he truly sets aside our sin to such a degree that it is as if we had never sinned at all. And this is because when he considers our sinfulness, he first considers Christ's righteousness—the righteousness of the one who took our sins upon himself and perfectly paid their penalty. "Who shall bring any charge against God's elect? It is God who justifies. Who is to condemn? Christ Jesus is the one who died—more than that, who was raised—who is at the right hand of God, who indeed is interceding for us" (Romans 8:33-34). We can have complete confidence that we have God's favor, so much confidence that our conscience can be as calm, as quiet, as undisturbed as if we had never sinned at all. And this is exactly the case, for God sees Christ in our place.

Though the patience of God be lasting,
yet it is not everlasting.

WILLIAM SECKER

Our God is wondrously patient with sinners, "gracious and merciful, slow to anger, and abounding in steadfast love; and he relents over disaster" (Joel 2:13). Yet we must be careful not to presume upon his patience or to expect that it will last for endless ages. For, as William Secker warns, "though the patience of God be lasting, yet it is not everlasting." A day is coming when God's patience will give away to judgment, for "he has fixed a day on which he will judge the world in righteousness by a man whom he has appointed" (Acts 17:31). This is why today—right now, at this very moment—God calls all to turn from their sin, to repent and believe in the gospel, for the day of judgment will come quickly and suddenly, like a thief in the night. Therefore, he says, "exhort one another every day, as long as it is called 'today,' that none of you may be hardened by the deceitfulness of sin" (Hebrews 3:13). Have you repented and believed? Don't delay, for God's patience may very soon turn to judgment.

THE DEEP AND DUE
CONSIDERATION OF THE
INFINITE PATIENCE OF GOD
TOWARDS US WILL GREATLY
PROMOTE THE PATIENCE OF
OUR SPIRITS, AND TRANSFORM
US INTO THE SAME IMAGE.

John Trapp

No attribute of God is without some application to human beings, and we do well to always consider how we can learn to honor and imitate our God in his perfections. As we consider God's mercy as expressed through patience, we ought to learn how we ourselves can express mercy through patience. As Trapp says here, "The deep and due consideration of the infinite patience of God toward us will greatly promote the patience of our spirits, and transform us into the same image." This indicates that the key to being patient toward others is considering the ways in which God has been patient with us. Said another way, if we find we lack patience toward others—if we are easily irritated, provoked over minor matters, or slow to be merciful and quick to be judgmental—then it indicates that we have failed to consider and appreciate God's patience toward us. The more we meditate on the ways in which God has been slow to anger and has abounded in steadfast love, the more our souls will be thrilled, the more our hearts will worship, and the more we will be drawn to imitate him.

GOD IS GOODNESS ITSELF, IN WHOM ALL GOODNESS IS INVOLVED. IF THEREFORE WE LOVE OTHER THINGS FOR THE GOODNESS WHICH WE SEE IN THEM, WHY DO WE NOT LOVE GOD, IN WHOM IS ALL GOODNESS? ALL OTHER THINGS ARE BUT SPARKS OF THAT FIRE, AND DROPS OF THAT SEA. IF YOU SEE ANY GOOD IN THE CREATURE, REMEMBER THERE IS MUCH MORE IN THE CREATOR. LEAVE THEREFORE THE STREAMS, AND GO TO THE FOUNTAINHEAD OF COMFORT. RICHARD SIBBES

We are naturally drawn to those who are good and who do good. We love those who love us, we appreciate those who are patient with us, we honor those who are merciful toward us. Richard Sibbes wants us to ensure we do not content ourselves with such derived goodness, but that we trace it to its source which is, of course, God himself. "If you see any good in the creature, remember there is much more in the Creator. Leave therefore the streams, and go to the fountainhead of comfort." Why drink from a murky stream when you could trace it to its source and drink from a sparkling spring? Why try to see dimly by the glow of a spark when you could see clearly by the light of a great fire? Why bathe in a bucket when you could swim in the sea? As you enjoy any goodness as expressed by human beings, be certain you don't neglect to revel in the source of all goodness—the God who himself is so very good.

GOD IS
TRUE

What does it mean that God is true? It certainly cannot mean less than that he is the one true God in a world of idols and fakes. There may be gods of wood and stone and vivid imagination, but he is the only one who is true and living. But it also means more than this. For God to be true is to indicate that he is the source and the standard of truth, so that something can only be considered true if it is consistent with what God thinks of it. Whenever a thought, idea, or conclusion is inconsistent with God's perspective, it must be false. Then it also means that God is reliable so that everything he says is correct and everything he promises will come to pass. And so we can have complete and total confidence in whatever God reveals of himself. If he says he is God, we can believe it; if he says he exists in the triune relationship of Father, Son, and Holy Spirit, we can believe it; if he says we are sinful, we can believe it; if he says he has sent his Son to save us from our sins, we can believe it; if he says he will return to judge the living and the dead, we can believe it. He is the true God who only ever speaks truly and who will undoubtedly prove to be true. In the short collection of quotes that follow, we will consider the one true God who loves us and who saves us.

[TRUTH] IS THAT ESSENTIAL PERFECTION OF HIS NATURE, *BY WHICH HE CANNOT BUT FULFILL* AND ACCOMPLISH WHATEVER HE HAS SPOKEN; *OR DO AS HE HAS SAID.*

—

JAMES FISHER

When we speak of God's truth, we refer to "that essential perfection of his nature, by which he cannot but fulfill and accomplish whatever he has spoken; or do as he has said." We often speak well of a person who is "true to his word," who does the things he has said he will do. We honor people who say, "My word is my bond." And in just that way, God is true—when he speaks, he utters no lie. When he speaks, he makes no promise he cannot or will not fulfill. When he speaks, we can have the highest confidence that he will do exactly what he has said precisely when he has said he will do it. Because God is perfect, it would be impossible for him to fail to come through on the least of his promises. "God is not man, that he should lie, or a son of man, that he should change his mind. Has he said, and will he not do it? Or has he spoken, and will he not fulfill it?" (Numbers 23:19). Of course not, for he is true.

The standard of true knowledge is conformity to God's knowledge. If we think the same thing God thinks about anything in the universe, we are thinking truthfully about it. Wayne Grudem

We live in a world in which the truth is not always apparent. We often have to weigh and consider competing options to determine which represents the truth and which represents an error or a lie. We hear that human life evolved through natural processes and that human life was created by God, and it falls to us to determine which is right and which is wrong. We hear that gender is a mere societal construct completely disconnected from biology and that gender is immutably related to God's design for male or female, and it falls to us to determine which is correct and which is incorrect. How can we know with any confidence? What is the standard to which we can appeal? Wayne Grudem answers well: "The standard of true knowledge is conformity to God's knowledge. If we think the same thing God thinks about anything in the universe, we are thinking truthfully about it." By his grace, God has opened up his mind for us and made it available through the Bible. It is here that we access true knowledge and develop true convictions.

THE
PROMISES
OF THE BIBLE ARE
NOTHING MORE THAN
GOD'S COVENANT TO BE
FAITHFUL TO HIS PEOPLE.
IT IS HIS CHARACTER
THAT MAKES THESE
PROMISES
VALID.

Jerry Bridges

The Bible is a book of promises, and those who read carefully will observe that in its pages God makes thousands and thousands of them. In its opening chapters he promises judgment upon those who rebel against him, then, when the first human beings do that very thing, he promises a Savior who will deliver them. In its middle chapters he promises to continue to bless his people and save them from their sin and sinfulness. In its closing pages he promises that Christ will soon return to judge the living and the dead and deliver the righteous to their wonderful reward. All of these promises can be summarized as Jerry Bridges does: "God's covenant to be faithful to His people." God tells us that he has set his love on his people and will surely fulfill his promised obligations to them. Of course, we have had many people make promises to us and then fail to come through. But we have no need to fear, for "it is His character that makes these promises valid." He will not fail to come through because he *cannot* fail to come through, for he is always true.

GOD WRITES WITH A PEN THAT NEVER BLOTS, SPEAKS WITH A TONGUE THAT NEVER SLIPS, ACTS WITH A HAND THAT NEVER FAILS.

Charles Spurgeon

We have already learned of God's wisdom and power, so we know that because God is wise, he always knows the best course of action, and because he is powerful, he always has the ability to bring it about. When we consider God's truth, we can have confidence that God always *will* bring it about. If he has promised an outcome, we can be absolutely certain he will achieve it; if he has promised mercy, we can be sure he will extend mercy; if he has promised judgment, we can be sure he will mete out judgment. For as Charles Spurgeon assures us, "God writes with a pen that never blots, speaks with a tongue that never slips, acts with a hand that never fails." If God is indeed true, it would be nothing short of impossible for him to plan imperfectly, to speak improperly, or to act impulsively. No, he will only ever decree, promise, and deliver in ways that are consistent with his truth. May we praise God, as did David, by saying "The sum of your word is truth, and every one of your righteous rules endures forever" (Psalm 119:160).

TRUTH IS WHAT GOD THINKS; IT IS WHAT GOD DOES; IT IS WHAT GOD IS; IT IS WHAT GOD HAS REVEALED OF HIMSELF IN THE BIBLE. TRUTH IS FOUND IN ITS FULLEST FORM IN GOD, FOR HE IS TRUTH; HE IS THE VERY SOURCE AND ORIGIN OF ALL TRUTH. **TIM CHALLIES**

"What is truth?" Pontius Pilate asked sarcastically (John 18:38). He, like so many others before and after, doubted that anyone could know the truth with any great certainty. Yet those who know God can indeed know the truth, for all that is true flows out of the one who is himself Truth. I trust you'll pardon me for quoting myself, but this quote from one of my older books gets at the matter quite well: "Truth is what God thinks; it is what God does; it is what God is; it is what God has revealed of himself in the Bible. Truth is found in its fullest form in God, for he is truth; he is the very source and origin of all truth." If we wish to know what is true, we will find that it is always perfectly aligned with the character, actions, and promises of God; if we wish to know what is false, we will find that it is always opposed by the characters, actions, and promises of God. God is true and truth, perfectly consistent and perfectly reliable in everything he says, everything he does, everything he promises.

There is many a believer who forsakes God, but there is never a believer whom God forsakes. Bob LaForge

Because God is true, he will come through on his every word and fulfill his every promise. And he has made some wonderful promises, such as "I will never leave you nor forsake you" (Hebrews 13:5), "I will give you rest" (Matthew 11:28), and "My power is made perfect in weakness" (2 Corinthians 12:9). He assures us that "all things work together for good, for those who are called according to his purpose" (Romans 8:28), that "he who raised the Lord Jesus will raise us also with Jesus and bring us with you into his presence" (2 Corinthians 4:14), and so much more besides. We may be prone to doubt God's promises because of our own failure to do what we have vowed—to be stalwart in our faith in Jesus Christ, to be committed in our love for others, to love God with our whole heart, soul, mind, and strength. Yet there is great joy and assurance in understanding that God does not revoke his promises simply because we fail to fulfill our own. "There is many a believer who forsakes God, but there is never a believer whom God forsakes." For God cannot forsake the ones to whom he has made such precious promises.

IN GOD'S FAITHFULNESS
LIES ETERNAL SECURITY.

Corrie ten Boom

One of the great promises that Christians can claim is the promise of security, that the God who saved us by his grace will never release us from his grip. If we have put our faith in Jesus Christ and been justified, we will surely also be sanctified and glorified, for these three can never be separated. The basis of our security is not our own ability, our own strength, or our own tenacity, and for that we give thanks to God, for we are not dependable, we are not trustworthy, we are not strong. If it depended upon us, we would surely all fall away and be lost. Corrie ten Boom reminds us of the wonderful news that "in God's faithfulness lies eternal security." The ground of our assurance is not any quality within us, but a precious attribute of the God who said, "Those whom he predestined he also called, and those whom he called he also justified, and those whom he justified he also glorified" (Romans 8:30). We can be confident that we will persevere to the end because God himself will preserve us.

What more powerful consideration can be thought on to make us true to God, *than the faithfulness and truth of God to us?*

William Gurnall

Though we will inevitably fail to be perfectly true to God, still the redeemed heart longs to grow in faithfulness, to be more consistent with truth, to be more like the God who has proven so very faithful and true. In that way, God's truth places both a desire and an obligation upon us, for as we have said, God's communicable attributes are not just to be admired but also imitated. We may wonder, is there a method we can use that will assist us? William Gurnall answers by way of a question: "What more powerful consideration can be thought on to make us true to God, than the faithfulness and truth of God to us?" The surest way for us to become increasingly true to God is to meditate upon his faithfulness and truth toward us. This then drives us to the pages of Scripture, where we see a God who was faithful to his Old Covenant people even when they spurned him, the one who toward us is "faithful and just to forgive us our sins and to cleanse us from all unrighteousness" (1 John 1:9), the one whose Son is "called Faithful and True" (Revelation 19:11).

CHRISTIANITY IS NOT SIMPLY A BODY OF TRUTH
TO BE BELIEVED; IT IS A SUPERNATURAL LIFE
THAT IS MEANT TO BE LIVED.

Crawford Loritts Jr.

As we come to the close of this section on the truth of God and draw near to the end of this book, it is important to remind ourselves that while the Christian faith is true and flows from the one who is himself Truth, this is not a faith that is meant to be merely believed. Rather, our beliefs are always meant to result in action. We put our faith in God and then live our lives for God. We believe the truth and then live out that truth before God and our fellow man. Crawford Loritts Jr. says it well: "Christianity is not simply a body of truth to be believed; it is a supernatural life that is meant to be lived." It is good and necessary to believe facts about God—facts that are revealed inerrantly and infallibly in the pages of Scripture. But God means for us to do something with those facts—to allow them to shape our character so we can live for his glory and the good of our neighbor. Then, and only then, will we be imitating the one who is the way, the truth, and the life.

CONCLUSION

I had the privilege of growing up under parents who valued family devotions—a daily time that included reading the Bible, praying, and then often considering a question and answer from a catechism. And while as a child I was always certain I had better things to do than this, when I became an adult, I realized I was profoundly thankful for the foundation it had laid. One of my clearest memories of these times is the day my father expressed his admiration for the Westminster Shorter Catechism and for the answer that has formed the basis of this book. He praised not only the content of the answer but also its rhythmic form. He told us he considered it one of the best uses of the English language he had ever encountered, and in that way, he helped teach me that truth can be both beautiful and said beautifully. In this book I have attempted to find some of the best examples of words that are not only true, but also stated in a way that is helpful, compelling, and perhaps even beautiful. For our beautiful God deserves no less. As we come to the final pages, I would like to offer just a few more words from the wise and a few more reflections on how our hearts should respond to this amazing God who is infinite, eternal, and unchangeable in his being, wisdom, power, holiness, justice, goodness, and truth.

THOMAS WATSON

IT IS LITTLE COMFORT TO KNOW THERE IS A GOD, UNLESS HE BE OURS . . . TO BE ABLE TO SAY, GOD IS MINE, IS MORE THAN TO HAVE ALL MINES OF GOLD AND SILVER.

There is great comfort in God. Of course, some people find comfort in gods as well. Rachel stole the family idols and carried them off so they could be hers. The Philistines captured the Ark of the Covenant and brought it into their temple so they could have its God and take advantage of his power. Each of them found comfort in the notion of having a god. But the true God is ours in a different way, a deeper way, a much better way. God is ours in a personal way—God the Father calls us, God the Son saves us, God the Spirit seals and sanctifies us. God adopts us into his family, makes us part of his body, and even takes up residence within us. God is ours not in the sense that we own him, but in the sense that he owns us and is joined to us by a bond that can never be broken. And to say the blessed words "God is mine" is far better than everything else this world has to offer, every treasure we can own, any jewel we can buy.

Real satisfaction comes not in understanding God's motives, but in understanding **His character**, in trusting in **His promises**, and in *leaning on Him* and *resting in Him* as the Sovereign who knows what He is doing and does all things well.

JONI EARECKSON TADA

For almost all of us, there will come times in life when we suffer, times when we grieve, times when God's providence decrees what we would never have chosen for ourselves. Some will meet these times, then rebel against God and abandon him, unwilling to accept that his will may involve their sorrow. It is only when we come to know the character of God that we can endure such times with joy and even with satisfaction. Joni Eareckson Tada has known much weakness and much pain, yet she can attest that "real satisfaction comes not in understanding God's motives, but in understanding His character, in trusting in His promises, and in leaning on Him and resting in Him as the Sovereign who knows what He is doing and does all things well." God's actions can never be separated from God's character, so when we know the latter, we can trust the former. To know God is to love him, and to know God is to trust him, even in the deepest and darkest valleys.

The Bible's message is worse than we like to think, in regard to our sin; but it is much better than we dream, in regard to our hope.

KATHLEEN NIELSON

Every one of the quotes in this book has been penned or spoken by someone who loves God and who honors his Word. In that way there is something of the Bible in each one of them. And the Bible communicates a message that is both far worse and far better than we could ever have imagined. It is far worse in its description of our sin and the divine demands of justice that sin necessitates. Yet it is far better in its description of the hope we can have despite our sin and sinfulness. Why? Because the Bible reveals a God who is far better than any we would ever have imagined or ever have fabricated. It reveals a God whose character is sublime and who only ever acts in ways that are consistent with it. It reveals a God who is perfect in every way, a God who is overflowing with love, grace, and mercy, a God who reaches out to humanity to offer us the precious gift of salvation. We, of all people, have hope because of the character of our God.

Worship is a believer's response
to God's revelation of Himself.

It is expressing
*wonder, awe, and
gratitude* for the *worthiness,*
the *greatness,* and the *goodness*
of our Lord.

—

NANCY DEMOSS WOLGEMUTH

God could have created us and then declined the opportunity to reveal himself to us. He could have set us loose on this earth without giving us any revelation of himself. He could have been the God who is there but who is silent. However, by his grace, he chose to reveal himself through his creation, through his Book, and through his Son. It is through such revelation that we come to know him as infinite, eternal, and unchangeable in his being, wisdom, power, holiness, justice, goodness, and truth. Such revelation is not to be met with silence or with apathy. Rather, it demands a response that involves the head, the heart, and the hands. We accept the fact of it on an intellectual level, we embrace it so it warms our hearts with joy and wonder, and we express it in our lives. In short, we allow God's revelation of himself to move us to worship. And it is my sincere hope, that through this collection of words from the wise, you will respond with worship, that you will express "wonder, awe, and gratitude for the worthiness, the greatness, and the goodness of our Lord."

ACKNOWLEDGMENTS

FROM TIM

I'd like to express my gratitude once again to Jules for working with me on another book, and to the team at Harvest House for their enthusiasm for this project. And of course, I'd like to express thankfulness to my family for their support.

FROM JULES

I'm grateful to the team at Harvest House for supporting us in our second book project together, to Tim for our years of creating graphics together for his engaging audience online, and to that audience whose excitement inspired us to create something that exists not only in a digital format but also as a tangible experience to share with others.

NOTES

1 Henry Smith, *The Works of Henry Smith* (Edinburgh: James Nichol, 1866), 1:80.

2 Cited in Jonathan Edwards, *The Works of Jonathan Edwards* (Ingersoll: Devoted Publishing, 2019), 2-3:42.

3 Andrew Gray, *A Door Opening into Everlasting Life* (Coconut Creek: Puritan Publications, 2013), 43.

4 Mark Jones, *God Is* (Wheaton: Crossway, 2017), Location 1024.

5 A.W. Tozer, *The Knowledge of the Holy* (New York: HarperCollins, 1978), 1.

6 Wayne Grudem, *Systematic Theology* (Leicester: IVP Press, 2004), 203.

SQUAREQUOTES CITATIONS

Page 6: F.F. Bruce, *The Gospel of John: Introduction, Exposition, Notes* (Grand Rapids, MI: Eerdmans, 1994), 105.

Page 8: William Strong, *Heavenly Treasure, or Man's Chiefest Good* (London: Printed by R.W. for Francis Tyton, 1656), 139.

Page 10: Charles Spurgeon, *Morning by Morning: A New Edition of the Classic Devotional Based on the Holy Bible, English Standard Version* (Wheaton, IL: Crossway Books, 2007), 178.

Page 12: Matthew Henry, *Commentary on the Whole Bible, vol. 4, Acts to Revelation* (Grand Rapids, MI: Christian Classics Ethereal Library, 1721), 1066.

Page 14: Jonathan Edwards, *The Experience That Counts* (Tain, UK: Christian Focus, 2016).

Page 16: Cited in John Blanchard, *The Complete Gathered Gold: A Treasury of Quotations for Christians* (Welwyn Garden City, UK: Evangelical Press, 2006).

Page 18: John Piper, *Desiring God* (Sisters, OR: Multnomah Books, 1996), 119.

Page 20: Vance Havner, *Holy Desperation: Finding God in Your Deepest Point of Need* (Washington, PA: CLC Publications, 2020).

Page 22: Jen Wilkin, *In His Image: 10 Ways God Calls Us to Reflect His Character* (Wheaton, IL: Crossway, 2018).

Page 24: Sam Storms, *Pleasures Evermore: The Life-Changing Power of Enjoying God* (Colorado Springs, CO: NavPress, 2000), 201.

Page 28: Peter C. Moore, *Disarming the Secular Gods: How to Talk So Skeptics Will Listen* (Westmont, IL: InterVarsity Press, 1989), 208.

Page 30: John MacArthur and Richard Mayhue, *Biblical Doctrine: A Systematic Summary of Bible Truth* (Wheaton, IL: Crossway Books, 2017).

Page 32: Robert M. Horn, *The Book That Speaks for Itself* (London, England: InterVarsity Press, 1969), 11.

Page 34: Cited in John Blanchard, *The Complete Gathered Gold: A Treasury of Quotations for Christians* (Welwyn Garden City, UK: Evangelical Press, 2006).

Page 36: William Lane Craig and Walter Sinnott-Armstrong, *God?: A Debate between a Christian and an Atheist* (New York, NY: Oxford University Press, 2004), 28.

Page 38: This quote is widely attributed to R.C. Sproul, though Ligonier Ministries is unable to confirm the source.

Page 40: Peter Du Moulin, *A Treatise of the Knowledge of God*, ed. C. Matthew McMahon and Therese B. McMahon (Coconut Creek, FL: Puritan Publications, 2013), 39.

Page 42: Cited in the Southern Baptist Theological Seminary, "Abstract of Principles," http://www.sbts.edu/about/abstract/.

Page 44: Thomas Goodwin, *Of the Creatures and the Condition of Their State by Creation* (Edinburgh, Scotland: James Nichol, 1863), 10.

Page 46: A.W. Tozer, *Knowledge of the Holy: Drawing Closer to God Through His Attributes* (Zeeland, MI: Reformed Church Publications, 2015).

Page 48: C.S. Lewis, "On Obstinacy in Belief," *The Sewanee Review* 63, no. 4 (1955): 525–38, http://www.jstor.org/stable/27538479.

Page 50: William Childs Robinson, "Summary of the Christian Faith According to the Shorter Catechism," *Southern Presbyterian Journal* (January 1950), https://www.pcahistory.org/HCLibrary/westminster/wcf/shorter/wcrobinson.pdf.

Page 54: Charles Spurgeon, "The Fourfold Treasure," *Metropolitan Tabernacle Pulpit vol. 17* (April 1871), https://www.spurgeon.org/resource-library/sermons/the-fourfold-treasure/#flipbook/.

Page 56: A.W. Tozer, *Knowledge of the Holy: Drawing Closer to God Through His Attributes* (Zeeland, MI: Reformed Church Publications, 2015).

Page 58: Matthew Newcomen, *The All-Seeing Unseen Eye of God and Other Sermons*, ed. C. Matthew McMahon and Therese B. McMahon (Coconut Creek, FL: Puritan Publications, 2013), 29.

Page 60: J.I. Packer, *Knowing God* (Downers Grove, IL: InterVarsity Press, 2021), 90.

Page 62: Isaac Watts, "Psalm 147 Part 1," https://hymnary.org/hymn/PHW/Ps.332.

Page 64: Matthew Henry, *Matthew Henry's Commentary on the Whole Bible, vol. 3* (Woodstock, Canada: Devoted Publishing, 2017), 206.

Page 66: Francis Haworth, *On Jacob's Ladder* (London, UK: G. Keith, 1762), 15.

Page 68: Mark Jones, *God Is: A Devotional Guide to the Attributes of God* (Wheaton, IL: Crossway, 2017), location 2205.

Page 70: Patrick Gillespie, *Gospel Standard* (London, UK: John Gadsby, 1882), 22.

Page 72: William Gurnall, *The Christian in Complete Armour* (London, UK: Blackie and Son, 1865), 109.

Page 74: J.I. Packer, *In God's Presence: Daily Devotions with J.I. Packer* (Wheaton, IL: Harold Shaw Publishers, 2000), 6.

Page 76: Cited in John Blanchard, *The Complete Gathered Gold: A Treasury of Quotations for Christians* (Welwyn Garden City, UK: Evangelical Press, 2006).

Page 80: A.W. Pink, *The Attributes of God* (Auckland, New Zealand: The Floating Press, 2009), 73.

Page 82: Jerry Bridges, *Trusting God* (Colorado Springs, CO: NavPress, 2016), 229.

Page 84: Jen Wilkin, *None Like Him: 10 Ways God Is Different from Us* (and Why That's a Good Thing) (Wheaton, IL: Crossway, 2016).

Page 86: Stephen Charnock, *Discourses upon the Existence and Attributes of God* (London, UK: W. Smith, 1797), 346.

Page 88: Thomas Brooks, *London's Lamentations* (London, UK: John Hancock and Nathaniel Ponder, 1670), 13.

Page 90: George Swinnock, *The Works of George Swinnock* (London, UK: James Nichol, 1868), 434.

Page 92: A.W. Pink, *The Attributes of God* (Auckland, New Zealand: The Floating Press, 2009), 63.

Page 94: John Greene, *The Fall of Adam and Other Works* (Coconut Creek FL: Puritan Publications, 2013), 56.

Page 96: R.C. Sproul, *Classic Teachings on the Nature of God* (Peabody, MA: Hendrickson, 2010), 172.

Page 98: Jerry Bridges, *The Practice of Godliness* (Colorado Springs, CO: NavPress, 2016), 113.

Page 100: Jeremy Taylor, *The Rule and Exercises of Holy Living* (London, UK: D. Brown, 1727), 199.

Page 102: A.W. Pink, *The Attributes of God* (Auckland, New Zealand: The Floating Press, 2009).

Page 106: Jen Wilkin, *In His Image: 10 Ways God Calls Us to Reflect His Character* (Wheaton, IL: Crossway, 2018).

Page 108: Sinclair Ferguson, *Devoted to God* (Carlisle, PA: Banner of Truth Trust, 2016), 107.

Page 110: A.W. Pink, *The Attributes of God* (Auckland, New Zealand: The Floating Press, 2009), 69.

Page 112: A.W. Pink, *The Attributes of God* (Auckland, New Zealand: The Floating Press, 2009), 64.

Page 114: Jonathan Edwards, *The Works of President Edwards in Four Volumes* (New York: Leavitt, Trow and Co., 1844), 103.

Page 116: Thomas Brooks, *The Crown and Glory of Christianity* (London, UK: H. Crips, 1662), 585.

Page 118: Matthew Henry, *An Exposition of the Book of Psalms* (London, UK: Bell & Daldy, 1866), 324.

Page 120: R.C. Sproul, *Choosing My Religion* (Phillipsburg, NJ: Presbyterian & Reformed, 2005).

Page 122: Oswald Chambers, *Biblical Ethics* (Grand Rapids, MI: Our Daily Bread Publishing, 2015).

Page 124: Jackie Hill Perry, *Holier Than Thou: How God's Holiness Helps Us Trust Him* (Nashville, TN: B&H Books, 2021), 2.

Page 126: J.C. Ryle, *Holiness* (Abbotsford, WI: Aneko Press, 2019), 10.

Page 128: Sinclair Ferguson, *Devoted to God* (Carlisle, PA: Banner of Truth Trust, 2016), 107.

Page 132: James Boyce, *Abstract of Systematic Theology* (Cape Coral, FL: Founders Press, 2006).

Page 134: Cited in James Montgomery Boice, *Whatever Happened to the Gospel of Grace?* (Wheaton, IL: Crossway Books, 2009), 104.

Page 136: John Stott, *The Cross* (Downers Grove, IL: InterVarsity Press, 2011), 67.

Page 138: Timothy Keller, *Romans 1–7 for You* (England, UK: Good Book Company, 2014).

Page 140: J.I. Packer and Mark Dever, *In My Place Condemned He Stood* (Wheaton, IL: Crossway Books, 2008), 89.

Page 142: Jen Wilkin, *In His Image: 10 Ways God Calls Us to Reflect His Character* (Wheaton, IL: Crossway, 2018).

Page 144: R.C. Sproul, *Classic Teachings on the Nature of God* (Peabody, MA: Hendrickson, 2010), 94.

Page 146: Charles Spurgeon, *The Metropolitan Tabernacle Pulpit* (London, UK: Passmore & Alabaster, 1875), 285.

Page 148: Matthew Henry, *An Exposition of All the Books of the Old and New Testaments* (London, UK: W. Baynes, 1804), 31.

Page 150: R.C. Sproul, *Classic Teachings on the Nature of God* (Peabody, MA: Hendrickson, 2010), 94.

Page 152: John Newton, *One Hundred and Twenty Letters from John Newton* (London, UK: Hamilton, Adams, and Co., 1847), 206.

Page 154: John Blanchard, *Whatever Happened to Hell?* (Darlington, UK: Evangelical Press, 1993), 101.

Page 158: Stephen Charnock, *Several Discourses upon the Existence and Attributes of God* (London, UK: D. Newman, 1682), 579.

Page 160: Wayne Grudem, *Systematic Theology* (Grand Rapids, MI: Zondervan, 2009), 198.

Page 162: Cited in John Blanchard, *The Complete Gathered Gold: A Treasury of Quotations for Christians* (Welwyn Garden City, UK: Evangelical Press, 2006).

Page 164: Cited in Steven J. Lawson, *Holman Old Testament Commentary*, vol. 10, *Job* (Nashville, TN: B&H Books, 2005), 183.

Page 166: Matthew Mead, *A Name in Heaven the Truest Ground of Joy* (London, UK: Edmund Parker, 1707), 30.

Page 168: Cited in Martin H. Manser, *The Westminster Collection of Christian Quotations* (Louisville, KY: Westminster John Knox Press, 2001), 137.

Page 170: John Henry Jowett, *Things That Matter Most* (Chicago, IL: Fleming H. Revell, 1913), 18.

Page 172: KB (@KB_HGA). Twitter Post, January 28, 2015, https://twitter.com/KB_HGA/status/560558517971861504.

Page 174: Jen Wilkin, *In His Image: 10 Ways God Calls Us to Reflect His Character* (Wheaton, IL: Crossway, 2018).

Page 176: Thomas Watson, *The Saint's Spiritual Delight, and, A Christian on the Mount* (London, UK: Religious Tract Society, 1830), 42.

Page 178: John Flavel, *The Fountain of Life Opened Up* (Woodstock, Canada: Devoted Publishing, 2018), 30.

Page 180: Matthew Henry, *Zondervan NIV Matthew Henry Commentary* (Grand Rapids, MI: Zondervan, 2010).

Page 182: Cited in John Howie, *The Scots Worthies* (Glasgow, Scotland: W.R. M'Phun, 1830), 337.

Page 184: William Secker, *The Nonsuch Professor in His Meridian Splendor* (London, UK: W. Nicholson, 1804), 188.

Page 186: Cited in John Blanchard, *The Complete Gathered Gold: A Treasury of Quotations for Christians* (Welwyn Garden City, UK: Evangelical Press, 2006).

Page 188: Richard Sibbes, *The Complete Works of Richard Sibbes*, D.D. (Edinburgh, Scotland: James Nichol, 1863), 282.

Page 192: James Fisher and Ebenezer Erskine, *The Assembly's Shorter Catechism Explained by Way of Question and Answer* (Belfast, Ireland: Daniel Blow, 1764), 50.

Page 194: Wayne Grudem, *Systematic Theology* (Grand Rapids, MI: Zondervan, 2009), 196.

Page 196: Jerry Bridges, *The Practice of Godliness* (Colorado Springs, CO: NavPress, 2016), 113.

Page 198: Charles Spurgeon, *The Treasury of David* (London, UK: Marshall Brothers, 1873), 105.

Page 200: Tim Challies, *The Discipline of Spiritual Discernment* (Wheaton, IL: Crossway Books, 2007), 94.

Page 202: Bob LaForge, *Contemplating the Almighty* (Perth Publishing, 1984), 120.

Page 204: Cited in Martin H. Manser, *The Westminster Collection of Christian Quotations* (Louisville, KY: Westminster John Knox Press, 2001), 128.

Page 206: William Gurnall, *The Christian in Complete Armour* (London, UK: L.B. Seeley, 1821), 155.

Page 208: Crawford W. Loritts Jr., *Unshaken: Real Faith in Our Faithful God* (Wheaton, IL: Crossway, 2015).

Page 212: Thomas Watson, *A Body of Practical Divinity* (Aberdeen, Scotland: D. Chalmers and Co., 1838), 51.

Page 214: Joni Eareckson Tada, *Is God Really in Control*, Joni and Friends, 1987, p. 9

Page 216: Kathleen Nielson, *Women and God: Hard Questions, Beautiful Truth* (Surrey, England: The Good Book Company, 2018).

Page 218: Nancy Leigh DeMoss, *A Place of Quiet Rest* (Chicago, IL: Moody, 2002).

ABOUT THE AUTHOR

Tim Challies is a Christian, a husband to Aileen, and a father to two daughters who are young adults and one son who is waiting for him in heaven. He worships and serves as an elder at Grace Fellowship Church in Toronto, Ontario. He is a blogger and book reviewer and has written a number of popular books. www.challies.com

ABOUT THE ILLUSTRATOR

Jules Koblun is the owner and creative lead at Goodwell Studio. She is a skilled thinker and maker, a dreamer and a visionary. When it comes to design, she is a compassionate guide and a passionate risk-taker. Jules has created SquareQuotes graphics for Tim Challies's blog since 2015. www.goodwellstudio.com